Sports Law in Belarus

Sports Law in Belarus

Aliaksandr Danilevich

This book was originally published as a monograph in the International Encyclopaedia of Laws/Sports Law.

Founding Editor: Roger Blanpain
General Editor: Frank Hendrickx
Volume Editor: Michele Colucci

Wolters Kluwer

Published by:
Kluwer Law International B.V.
PO Box 316
2400 AH Alphen aan den Rijn
The Netherlands
E-mail: lrs-sales@wolterskluwer.com
Website: www.wolterskluwer.com/en/solutions/kluwerlawinternational

Sold and distributed by:
Wolters Kluwer Legal & Regulatory U.S.
7201 McKinney Circle
Frederick, MD 21704
United States of America
E-mail: customer.service@wolterskluwer.com

ISBN 978-94-035-4911-8

e-Book: ISBN 978-94-035-4672-8
web-PDF: ISBN 978-94-035-4433-5

The Author

Dr Aliaksandr Danilevich was born in 1974 in Minsk, Belarus; he graduated from the Law Faculty of the Belarusian State University in 1996. Currently, he is an Associate Professor at the Belarusian State University in Minsk. As an independent arbitrator, he has engaged in legal practice as a member of the Minsk City Bar. His practice is in international commercial arbitration, international litigation and sports law. He is a member of the Court of Arbitration for Sport in Lausanne, the International Arbitration Court at the Belarusian Chamber of Commerce and Industry and several other arbitration institutions.

The Author

Table of Contents

List of Abbreviations

BYN	Belarusian Roubles
CC	Civil Code
CCP	Code of Civil Procedure
CEP	Code of Economic Procedure
CIS	Commonwealth of Independent States
ETA	European Tennis Association
FHRB	Federation of Ice Hockey of Republic of Belarus
IOC	International Olympic Committee
IIHF	International Ice Hockey Federation
ITF	International Tennis Federation
LC	Labour Code
LPCS	Law on Physical Culture and Sport
NADA	National Anti-Doping Agency
NOC	National Olympic Committee
PC	Paralympic Committee
TC	Tax Code
UN	United Nations
USSR	Union of Soviet Socialist Republics
UNCITRAL	United Nations Commission on International Trade Law
WADA	World Anti-Doping Agency

Preface

Belarus has its own legislation on sports that has a strong administrative impact. This phenomenon has its roots in the country's Soviet heritage when the state regulated sports relations as part of the public sector. In Belarus, the Ministry of Sports and Tourism makes rules on sporting activity in the country according to national sports law. National and local sports federations and the National Olympic Committee are autonomous, but they act in close coordination with the Ministry of Sports and Tourism. State financing determines the strict regulation of the organization of sports competitions, sports activities in schools and the participation of national teams in international tournaments. Belarus has signed international conventions on anti-doping issues and fights against hooliganism and misbehaviour in stadiums.

The academic interest in sports law has increased manifold over the past five years. The sports law discipline has become part of the study programme in many law faculties. Many articles have been written and many changes have taken place in legislation, but the principle of the administrative regulation of sports is still reserved.

Acknowledgements

This monograph would not have been possible without the support and encouragement of my wife, Volha, who encouraged me to focus during a long period of writing. I also would like to express my gratitude to my legal assistant, Katsiaryna Shyshova, who provided technical assistance, helped translate many parts to English and facilitated an update in 2021.

Acknowledgements

General Introduction

1. According to its Constitution, Belarus is a democratic social state functioning under the rule of law (Article 1 of the Constitution of the Republic of Belarus). Article 8 of the Belarusian Constitution admits the priority of generally acknowledged principles of international law and assures the conformity of legislation therewith. Foreign citizens and persons without citizenship in Belarus enjoy the rights and freedoms and carry duties equally with the citizens of Belarus unless otherwise provided for by the Constitution, Laws and International Treaties (Article 11 of the Constitution).

2. The state power is divided into legislative, executive and judicial branches. Belarus is a presidential republic. The President is the head of state and the guarantor of the Constitution and of the people's rights and freedoms. In accordance with the Constitution, the Parliament acts as a legislative body, consisting of two chambers. The executive power in the republic is relegated to the Government, with the Council of Ministers being the central body of state administration.

3. Local administration and self-administration are carried out through a system of local executive and administrative bodies, bodies of self-administration and referenda.

4. The judicial power in the republic belongs to the courts. Control over the accordance of legal acts within the Constitution is relegated to the Constitutional Court of the Republic of Belarus.

§1. State System

5. According to its Constitution, the Republic of Belarus is a unitary, democratic social state based on the rule of law. The Constitution currently in force in the Republic of Belarus was adopted in 1994, with subsequent amendments and additions adopted at national referenda on 24 November 1996 and 17 October 2006.

6. The President of the Republic of Belarus is the head of state. The Parliament – the National Assembly – is the representative and legislative body of the Republic of Belarus. The Parliament consists of two chambers: the House of Representatives (110 deputies) and the Council of the Republic (64 members).

7. Executive power in the Republic of Belarus is exercised by the Council of Ministers of the Republic of Belarus, which is headed by the Prime Minister.

8. State power in the Republic of Belarus is exercised on the principle of division of powers among the legislature, the executive and the judiciary branches. State bodies are independent within the confines of their powers; they cooperate among themselves, acting on the principle of checks and balances.

9. Supervision of the constitutionality of the state's legislative enactments is exercised by the Constitutional Court of the Republic of Belarus.

I. The Parliament

10. As mentioned above, the Parliament – the National Assembly – is the representative and legislative body of Belarus. The Parliament consists of two chambers: the House of Representatives and the Council of the Republic.

11. The House of Representatives consists of 110 deputies. The election of deputies to the House of Representatives is carried out in accordance with the law on the basis of universal, equal, free and direct electoral suffrage and by secret ballot.

12. The Council of the Republic is a chamber of territorial representation. The Council of the Republic consists of eight deputies from every region and the city of Minsk, elected at the meetings of local Councils of Deputies in every region and the city of Minsk from their respective ranks. Eight members of the Council of the Republic are nominated by the President.

13. Elections for a new composition of the chambers of Parliament are to be set no later than four months and to be held no later than thirty days prior to the expiry of the powers of the current Parliament.

14. Extraordinary elections for the chambers of the Parliament are to be held within three months of the premature expiry of the powers of the chambers of the Parliament.

II. The Government

15. According to Article 106 of the Belarusian Constitution, the executive power in Belarus shall be exercised by the Government; more specifically, by the Council of Ministers of the Republic of Belarus, the central body of state administration.

16. The Government shall be accountable for its actions to the President and is responsible to the Parliament. The Government shall relinquish its powers to the President-elect.

17. The Government shall consist of the Prime Minister, his deputies and Ministers. The heads of other central bodies of state administration may be members of the Government.

18. The Prime Minister shall be appointed by the President of the Republic of Belarus with the consent of the House of Representatives. The decision in this matter shall be made by the House of Representatives within two weeks from the nomination of the candidacy of the Prime Minister. If the House of Representatives rejects the submitted nomination of the Prime Minister twice, the President may appoint an acting Prime Minister, dissolve the House of Representatives and call new elections.

19. The Government or any member therein shall be entitled to tender their resignation to the President if they deem it impossible to discharge the duties entrusted to them. The Government shall also tender its resignation to the President if the House of Representatives has passed a vote of no confidence to the Government.

20. The Prime Minister may request from the House of Representatives a vote of no confidence with regard to the Governmental Programme or any other issue submitted to the House. If a vote of no confidence is passed by the House of Representatives, the President shall be entitled to accept the resignation of the Government or dissolve the House of Representatives within ten days and call for new elections. If the resignation of the Government is rejected, it shall continue to discharge its duties.

21. The President shall be entitled to make the decision with respect to the resignation of the Government or the dismissal of any member of the Government on his own initiative.

22. In case of the resignation of the Government of Belarus or the termination of its powers, it shall continue to hold office as instructed by the President until a new Government is formed.

23. The Government of Belarus shall have the right to pass legislative acts that have binding force in the entire territory of the Republic of Belarus. The Prime Minister shall issue orders that are under his jurisdiction. The competence of the Government and the procedure governing its activities shall be determined on the basis of the Constitution and the Law on the Council of Ministers of the Republic of Belarus.

III. The Ministry of Sports and Tourism

24. The Ministry of Sports and Tourism of Belarus is a republican state body and reports to the Council of Ministers of Belarus. The Ministry of Sports and Tourism creates state policy in the field of physical training, sport and tourism and coordinates activities in these spheres for other republican state bodies. Its activity is regulated by the decision of the Council of Ministers of Belarus from 29 July 2006, No. 963 (updated version: 24 February 2021), 'Matters of the Ministry of Sports and Tourism of Belarus'.[1]

25. Duties of the Ministry of Sports and Tourism in the sporting sphere are:

(1) Carrying out state policies in the fields of physical training and sport and coordinating activities in these spheres for other republican state bodies.
(2) Realizing state regulations in the fields of sport, sport-improvement and tourist activity and creating conditions for the development of organizations of all patterns of ownership that are carrying out given types of economic activities.
(3) Realizing training regulations for sports reserves and competitive sportspeople, including coordinating the organization of training of sports reserves and competitive sportspeople in organizations of different types, irrespective of department affiliations and form of ownership.
(4) Designing government programmes to develop physical training, sport and tourism and inter-branch coordination of their performance.
(5) Creating scientifically proven systems of physical training and improvement for the population and the training of sports reserves for higher achievements.
(6) Creating a research base and perfecting the system of scientifically methodical maintenance of activities in the field of physical training, sport and tourism together with interested organizations.
(7) Organizing and conducting domestic and international sport and tourist events within the territory of Belarus.
(8) Maintaining the preparation of the national teams of Belarus and their participation in international sports events together with interested organizations.
(9) Developing propaganda for physical training, sport and tourism and healthy ways of life through the issue of print sources, guidance papers, visual materials, promotional videos, publications, posters and stands.
(10) Providing assistance to republican and other public associations in their activities related to physical training, sport and tourism.
(11) Participating in the formation and realization of state policy regarding the creation of material resources for physical training, sport and tourism.
(12) Monitoring the implementation of Belarusian legislation in physical training, sport and tourism.
(13) Coordinating activities for specialized educational sports institutions, including sports institutions for children and young people (specialized institutions for Olympic reserves for children and young people), which are included in the structure of sports clubs by way of separate subdivisions, and determining the duration and order of organization, realization and other peculiarities of the training process.
(14) Providing training support and personnel development;
(15) Carrying out the overall direction of doping control.

1. The National Register of Legal Acts of Belarus, 14 Aug. 2006, No. 127, 5/22683.

26. The Ministry of Sports and Tourism conducts the following core functions in the sphere of the development of physical training and sport:

(1) Participating in the draft preparation of acts and standard legal acts of the Government of Belarus and developing and accepting standard legal acts and methodical instructions concerning physical training, sports and tourism.
(2) Organizing the development and realization of corresponding government programmes and actions, analysing the course of their performance and informing on it to the President of Belarus and the Council of Ministers of Belarus.
(3) Carrying out state personnel selection, directed at deploying the administrative duties of the Ministry of Sports and Tourism and the agencies within the Ministry of Sports and Tourism system, with focus on highly qualified specialists; ensuring the placement of these specialists; encouraging competence within its senior personnel and its reserve; creating a departmental system of continuous personnel training and organizing the training of specialists with higher and dual education.
(4) Developing schedules of pay-rate characteristics by the trades and roles of workers within physical training, sports and tourism.
(5) Providing opportunities for the improvement of professional skills and the retraining of experts in the sphere of physical training, sports and tourism.
(6) Defining, in coordination with the Ministry of Labour and Social Protection and the Ministry of Finance, feature calculations for the work experience of speciality (in branch) workers in physical training and sport.
(7) Confirming an order of the admission of citizens to pedagogical activities in the physical training and sports sphere and an order for the passage of citizens who have undergone special preparation for admission to employment in pedagogical activities in the physical training and sports sphere.
(8) Creating budgetary and non-budgetary development funds in accordance with Belarusian legislation.
(9) Organizing domestic and international conferences, congresses, meetings and seminars concerning physical training, sport and tourism, participating in the work of interstate and intergovernmental organizations and public associations conducting activities that infringe on the interests of the Ministry of Sports and Tourism and representing the interests of Belarus at international sports organizations and in sports and other actions conducted by international sports organizations.
(10) Developing and confirming the planned domestic schedule of official sports competitions and training and the gathering and participation of the national teams of Belarus in international activities; conducting sport-improving and tourist actions within the territory of Belarus, coordinating domestic and international competitions and gatherings and cooperating on a voluntary basis with ministries and other state bodies, organizations and public associations.
(11) Developing and confirming the Uniform Sport Classification of Belarus and registering the sports records of Belarus.
(12) Forming structured national teams for Belarus and providing for their preparation and participation in international sports events.

(13) Controlling the correctness of applications for the list of sports eligible for professional pension insurance, including the separate categories of sportspeople engaged in professional sport, the rules on the criteria for estimating the working conditions for separate categories of workers and (or) types of work carried out for professional pension insurance and the order of their application, as confirmed by the decision of the Council of Ministers of Belarus on 9 October 2008, No. 1490 (updated version: 24 June 2016, 'About Some Questions of Professional Pension Insurance'[2]), concerning sportspeople.
(14) Establishing the list of sports constructions that are the basis for preparing the national and international teams of Belarus.
(15) Confirming regulations on sports judges, including an order of special preparation of sports judges in the organizations of physical training and sport responsible for refereeing the official sports competitions of Belarus.
(16) Organizing the official championship draws in Belarus.
(17) Defining an order for the deprivation of the right to participate in the official sports competitions of Belarus and in the national teams of Belarus for sportspeople who violate anti-doping rules, persons guilty of encouraging sports people to violate anti-doping rules and the sportspeople who have refused anti-doping control.
(18) Certifying the assignment of the status of national sports federations and establishing an order relating to conducting the register of national federations.
(19) Developing and confirming, when due hereunder, the regulations on domestic sport ranks and defining an order for assigning qualifying categories to coaches and teachers of sport and other categories of workers in the physical training and sports sphere.
(20) Defining an order of delivery of prizes to winners and participants of sports competitions and payments of compensation to the coaches who take part in their preparation.
(21) Managing domestic competitions and approving their regulations.
(22) Developing sport ranks and awards within their competence for medals, counters, badges, diplomas, prizes of winners of domestic sports competitions; coaches; physical training, sport and tourism workers; and the active workers and veterans of sports movements, and other physical training, sport and tourist organizations and clubs.
(23) Deciding on nominee representation for the special award of the President of Belarus the 'Belarus Sport Olympus' and, when due hereunder, confirming drawings of the winner of the award and the honourable medal of the winner of this special award.
(24) Presiding over the preparations of sports reserves, coordinating the development of specialized sporting schools, irrespective of their subordination, and supervising the training processes within them.
(25) Adopting regulations for specialized sports establishments and their branches, city and regional sport-improving centres (centres for sport-improving work), sports clubs and sports camps; making orders on the design of sports camps,

2. The National Register of Legal Acts of Belarus, 2008, No. 249, 5/28508.

including the organization of training processes, the direction of sports coaches and the state accreditation and certification of specialized sports establishments.

(26) Adopting regulations for high schools acting as schools for Olympic reserves.

(27) Ordering the creation and activity of collective physical training of the organization.

(28) Defining the instructions for the organizing and granting of paid sport-improving services.

(29) Establishing the classification of sports constructions and defining the basic requirements for their work.

(30) Establishing daily food norms for pupils attending schools for Olympic reserves and the daily provisions for the pupils of specialized sports schools and Olympic reserve schools when training in sports camps, when due hereunder.

(31) Establishing orders for the reception, transfer, deduction and restoration of specialized sports establishments.

(32) Defining the number of persons that may be accepted (acquisition plans) to specialized sports schools on free-payment conditions, financed at the expense of the republican budget; defining acquisition plans by type of sport at Olympic reserve schools; estimating the number of persons received at establishments providing average special and higher education, financed by means of the republican budget.

(33) Managing the state accreditation of specialized sports establishments and the state certification of centres for Olympic reserves and centres of Olympic preparation.

(34) Carrying out the general management of population-level physical training and preparation of sportspeople, ensuring, in cooperation with local executive and administrative bodies and other state agencies, the exercise of governmental regulations and administration in the sporting sphere and managing the fitness and health recreation information dispensed to the public, in fulfilment of state fitness and health recreation goals of Belarus.

(35) Developing specifications for physical readiness for various categories of the population.

(36) Coordinating the rules of sports competitions by sport type.

(37) Coordinating the development of scientific activities and confirming programmes of scientific research on problems within physical training, sport and tourism.

(38) Providing consideration for and, when due hereunder, the issue of educational, methodical documentation and literature concerning physical training, sport and tourism.

(39) Conducting scientifically methodical preparation and medical maintenance for the national teams of Belarus and sports reserves in conjunction with interested organizations and associations.

(40) Adopting rules and specifications for material, regenerative and pharmacological maintenance, food and expenses for the organizations conducting and participating in sporting events; the typical states and specifications for the number of physical training and sports organizations, schools for Olympic

reserves and national teams; the monetary norms of food expenses for pupils of specialized sporting schools and pupils of Olympic reserves training in sports camps and the typical states and specifications of the number of physical training and sports organizations and schools for Olympic reserves, in coordination with the Ministry of Finance.

(41) Defining an order of material support for the national teams of Belarus in coordination with the Ministry of Finance.

(42) Defining an order of maintenance of sport-improving centres, sports clubs, area commands, cities and regional areas for participation in domestic sport, mass sport and tourist events.

(43) Adopting safety rules for conducting employment in physical training and sports activities, in coordination with the Ministry of Internal Affairs, and developing safety rules for conducting sports events on roads for general use.

(44) Adopting rules on the qualifying commissions and specifications of the number of sports instructors and the sporting work of organizations.

(45) Carrying out the general management of the anti-doping control organization in the field of sport.

(46) Cooperating with local executive and administrative bodies on economic, social and other decisions and working with regional and Minsk City executive committees on activity perfection in the development of physical training, sport and tourism.

(47) Coordinating positions within the physical training, sport and tourism departments in regional and Minsk City executive committees.

(48) Managing the activities of state organizations subordinated to the Ministry of Sports and Tourism and, partially:

  (a) Adopting the charters of given organizations and making appointments to posts and demotions.

  (b) Controlling the efficiency of use and safety of state property.

  (c) Making decisions on the creation of such organizations and on their reorganization and liquidation.

  (d) Determining economic specifications for the efficiency of managing and conducting uniform economic policies in corresponding spheres for addressing these specifications and maintaining control over their application.

  (e) Coordinating foreign trade activities for given organizations to increase the efficiency and competitiveness of the export of services in the sphere of physical training, sport and tourism.

  (f) Maintaining the performance of target indicators of export forecasts, imports and the balance of foreign trade in the sphere of physical training, sport and tourism.

(49) Carrying out the following powers in the field of labour safety:

  (a) Governing labour safety at the branch level.

  (b) Working out and accepting, within the competence of branch rules on labour safety, the typical instructions on labour safety and other standard legal acts, including the technical standard legal acts containing the requirements on labour safety; working out and realizing branch target programmes to improve conditions and labour safety.

(c) Controlling the observance of labour safety requirements in the state organizations subordinated to the Ministry of Sports and Tourism.
(d) Analysing the results of the certification of working conditions, the certification of sanitary-engineering conditions and labour safety and the reasons for industrial traumatism and professional diseases in state organizations subordinated to the Ministry of Sports and Tourism; determining and realizing measures for their preventive maintenance.
(e) Organizing training for the improvement of professional skills and examinations concerning the labour safety knowledge of the heads and experts of the state organizations subordinated to the Ministry of Sports and Tourism.
(f) Conducting research work in the field of conditions and labour safety.
(g) Providing information to the state organizations subordinated to the Ministry of Sports and Tourism concerning labour safety.
(h) Developing and distributing propaganda regarding best practices in the field of labour safety to the state organizations subordinated to the Ministry of Sports and Tourism.
(i) Ensuring international cooperation within the competencies concerning labour safety.
(j) Other powers in the field of labour safety, as provided for by the legislation.

(50) Considering, within the competence of an order established by the legislation, the reference (offer, statement, complaint) of citizens, including individual businesspeople and legal bodies (hereinafter ‘references’).
(51) Providing specified organizations with obligatory instructions for the execution of appropriate decisions when the authors are not satisfied with the results of their consideration by the system of the Ministry of Sports and Tourism.
(52) Providing the heads of Ministry of Sports and Tourism subordinate establishments with instructions on bringing to justice those officials who fail to deal properly with complaints and citizen communications.
(53) Controlling the activities of system organizations within the Ministry of Sports and Tourism by regulating their activities and exercising relevant powers through the analysis of the efficiency of the system organization and the development of proposals for its improvement, within its competence.
(54) Carrying out lottery activities, when due hereunder.
(55) Ensuring the organizations conducting tourist activities observe the requirements of technical standard legal acts in the field of technical rationing and the standardization of the quality of tourist services.
(56) Controlling:
(a) The state cadastre of tourist resources of Belarus.
(b) The national register of guides and guide-translators of Belarus.
(c) The register of sport types.
(d) The register of national sports federations.
(e) The book of comments and suggestions.

(57) Defining the order of rule observance on the personal safety of tourists.
(58) Confirming the form of receipt on excursion services.

(59) Informing subjects and participants of tourist activities on the countries (places) they are visiting that present safety threats for tourists, by means of placing corresponding data in republican mass media.
(60) Developing projects and preparing offers on the conclusion of international contracts with foreign states.
(61) Purchasing goods (works, services) at the expense of the republican budget, within the estimates for the next financial (budgetary) year, when due hereunder.
(62) Appointing and paying state grants to Olympic champions and Presidential grants in the sporting sphere to sportspeople and coaches of national teams, giving out prizes in monetary or other forms to sportspeople who have achieved high sports results and remunerating coaches who have participated in the training of such sportspeople.
(63) Carrying out other functions according to the legislation.

Cooperating with the mass media promotes information on the global computer network internet in order to cover issues related to the activities of the Ministry of Sports, with the exception of information, the dissemination and (or) presentation of which is limited (6.26-1).

Defining the main areas of activity in the field of fire safety, developing comprehensive fire-fighting measures that are important for the industry or several objects, exercising other powers in this area, as well as in the field of protecting the population and territories from natural and man-made emergencies, carrying out state regulation in the field of industrial safety within the powers provided for by legislative acts (6.28).

§2. Introduction to the Legal System of the Republic of Belarus

27. The State tradition in Belarus is a long one: the Statute of the Grand Duchy of Lithuania, Russia and Zhamoitian, the third edition of which was published in 1588 in the old Belarusian language, was the only full code of law in Europe since Roman law until the Napoleonic Code was adopted in 1804. The Statute has been edited several times and it determined the legal system of the Duchy for about 250 years until it was abolished by the Moscovian Tsar. The Statute was a comprehensive and elaborate code of laws on the state, civil, criminal and procedural rules of the Grand Duchy, which had the highest legal force within the territory of the country.

28. The legal system of any state includes objective laws reflecting the development of society and its historical, national and cultural peculiarities. Belarus, like any other state, has its own legal system, which has both features common to the legal systems of other countries and its own special characteristics. The legal system of Belarus, as well as the legal systems of other states of continental Europe, belongs to the Romano–Germanic law family.

29. The Constitution of Belarus is the fundamental law and has supreme legal force. Laws, ordinances of the President, decrees of the President and other acts of state bodies (officials) are adopted and enacted in compliance with the Constitution.

Part I. Organization of Sport

Chapter 1. General Issues

30. The Law on Physical Culture and Sport (LPCS) of the Republic of Belarus establishes the core concepts of sports relations in Article 1, where the following basic terms are used:

(1) Physical training: the compound part of the general culture, the sphere of welfare based on spiritual and material assets, created and used by society with a view to the physical development of the person, perfecting the impellent activity, strengthening the health and promoting the harmonious development of the person.
(2) Sport: a sphere of activity; a combination of sports has developed in the form of sports competitions and training for them.
(3) Sports education: an integrated process aimed at the physical development and the improvement of skills and knowledge in the field of physical culture and sports to form a comprehensively developed and physically healthy person, including physical preparation.
(4) Physical preparation: the process of using the tools, techniques, forms and conditions of exercise that directly influence the physical development of the human.
(5) Sportsperson: an individual exercising sports training in the chosen sport.
(6) Sports club: a voluntary association of individuals, without registering as a legal entity, created by an organization to prepare for fitness and health, sports events and sports competitions and participate in them.
(7) Sports actions: sports competitions and the preparation for them.
(8) Sports constructions: the objects intended for conducting physical training and sports activities.

31. According to Article 6 of the LPCS, the Olympic movement of Belarus is a part of the international Olympic movement, the objectives of which include promoting and implementing the principles of the Olympic movement, promoting the development of physical culture and sport, the strengthening of international cooperation in the sphere of physical culture and sport and representing Belarus in the Olympics and other international sports events held under the auspices of the International Olympic Committee (IOC), the European Olympic Committees and the Association of National Olympic Committees.

32. Article 7 of the LPCS provides a definition for the Paralympic movement of Belarus, which is part of the international Paralympic movement, the objectives of which are to promote the development of the physical culture of sportspeople with disabilities, to strengthen international cooperation in the sphere of physical culture and sport and to represent Belarus at the Paralympic Games and other international sports events held with the participation of the above-mentioned persons.

33. According to Article 1 of the LPCS, attaining higher achievements is part of the sport and includes sportspeople achieving high results when participating in official domestic sports competitions and official international sporting events. Article 53 of the LPCS states that the state provides the conditions for developing high-performance sports by financing sports reserves and high-class sportspeople, establishing links with international sports organizations, forming the national sporting teams of Belarus and providing them with training, helping in the organization of sports activities in the territory of the Republic of Belarus and ensuring the participation of sportspeople of Belarus in international sports competitions and other means. The President of Belarus establishes:

(1) the size of prizes for sportspeople who win medals at the Olympics, Paralympics and Deaflympics;
(2) the size of rewards for coaches who provided training for these sportspeople;
(3) the number, size, method of appointment and payment of scholarships of the President of Belarus in the sphere of physical culture and sports;
(4) the size, order of appointment and payment of public Olympic champions' scholarships.

34. The LPCS regulates the concept of 'professional sport' in Article 55:

> Professional sport is the part of sport that includes commercial, labour and other activities not forbidden by the legislation directed to the achievement of high sports results and the reception of compensation (incomes) through the organization of sport actions and (or) participation in them. The relations arising in professional sport between natural persons and (or) legal entities who are carrying out activities in the professional sphere are regulated by the CC of Belarus, the Labour Code (LC) of Belarus, the LPCS and other legislation.

35. If an international contract of Belarus establishes rules other than those contained in the present Law, the norms of the international contract are applied (Article 2 LPCS).

§1. General Principles

36. Principles of law or branches of the legislation are the basis for the structure of the law. Legal norms, institutes and law and legislation branches cannot contradict the principles of law. Within the limits of sports law, it is possible to allocate branch principles to its separate institutes.

37. It is impossible to confuse the principles of sports law (principles of the legal regulation of sports relations) with the principles or problems of the state regulation of physical training and sport (state policy) established by the law. Despite the presence of a uniform subject of regulation, the concept of the state principles of sports regulation is wider, as the issue of statutory acts regulating sports relations is part of the state support of sports. The state carries out a policy of supporting sport by creating favourable conditions for financing sports organizations, the continuity of physical training and the interests of citizens by developing and realizing programmes to improve physical training and sport (Article 9 LPCS). One of the state's means of realizing policy in the field of physical training and sport is the creation of corresponding rules of law by competent state organizations. Thus, state policy principles influence the formation of sports law principles.

38. The system of sports law principles consists of both general and special sports law principles. The general principles of sport are those inherent only in the right to sport, within the specific subject of regulation. Special principles regulate separate institutions of sports law and are the administrative norms used in civil, labour, enterprise and international law. Accordingly, in the regulation of these institutions, the principles regulating the granted rights of the branches and their institutes are used.

39. The principle of the general right to practice sport includes two interconnected rights – the right to practice physical training and sport and the inadmissibility of discrimination during the realization of such a right. The right to employment in physical training and sport is established by the national sports legislation. The greatest value of this principle is for amateur (mass amateur) sport. According to Article 4 of the Belarus LPCS, 'Each citizen of Belarus has the right to physical training and sport.' The right of citizens of Belarus to physical training and sport is provided by the state through the creation of necessary conditions for its realization, carrying out state policy in the sphere of physical training and sport. Article 4 of the LPCS also establishes a principle of national (equal) treatment for foreign citizens and persons without citizenship in the physical training and sport sphere: 'Foreign citizens and persons without citizenship in the territory of Belarus enjoy the rights in a physical training and sport sphere equally with citizens of Belarus if not otherwise defined by the Constitution of Belarus, the present Law, other laws and the international contracts of Belarus.'

40. If the legislation of Belarus does not provide exceptions to national treatment for foreigners as mentioned in Article 4 of the LPCS, any restrictions established by national sports federations on the participation of foreigners in national championships are unlawful.

41. The principle of legal protection of sportspeople: A sportsperson, as well as other physical persons, possess a set of rights provided by the Constitution. However, features of the sports law, in particular at the initial stages of sports commercialization, have led to the necessity of protecting sportspeople's rights. The best example is the development of sports rights within the limits of EU law. EU law, namely the practices of the European Court of Justice, has affected the entrance of new norms into national legislation on sport. To protect labour rights, sportspeople and coaches have the right to form trade unions and associations and enter into social dialogue with clubs and their associations as employers.

42. The principle of the relative autonomy of sport: Being a cultural component, sport cannot and should not be completely settled by the state. The overwhelming majority of rules for competitions are regulated by sports laws – the acts of sports federations. This mostly concerns professional sports.

43. In a broad sense, autonomy is understood as the competence to settle relations within the limits of own competence and the following of established rules, particularly in questions of doping or other responsibilities.[3] However, sports autonomy is not absolute, as the state and supranational structures (within the limits of the EU) actively interfere with the regulation of sports relationships. On the one hand, such intervention occurs first in the realization of the principle of protecting sportspeople's rights that are well looked through on jurisprudence of the European Court of Justice. On the other hand, the state's participation in sports regulation is not always through the establishment of restrictive legal frameworks of activity for sports organizations.

44. Sports autonomy derives from the certain autonomy of sports federations, and it is established in the legislation. Formation of sports federations is the realization of the right by citizens to create public organizations (associations). A national federation can be formed as an association if it is not forbidden by the legislation. Article 3(3) of the European Sports Charter of 1992 defines that, 'the voluntary sport organizations have the right to form independent mechanisms on decision-making within the limits of the law. Both the governmental and sports organizations should recognize [the] necessity of mutual respect of their decisions'.

45. However, as noted at the start of researching the given principle, the subjective defines the autonomy of sport, as well as the objective. Sports have huge social and cultural value. Due to the special social status of professional sports, it is impossible and unnecessary to automatically apply all principles of legal regulation in administrative and civil law.

46. In conclusion, it is necessary to notice that the balance of the principles of autonomy of sport and the principle of protecting the rights of sportspeople is the basis for the progressive development of the right to sport as a whole.

47. The principle of fair competition: The given principle at first sight concerns only the behaviour of sportspeople (fair play), though it is not limited to this.

---

3. Vieweg., K. The Legal Autonomy of Sport Organization and the Restrictions of European Law // Professional Sport in the EU: Regulation and Re-regulation. / Caiger, A.; Gardiner, S. – 1st ed. – The Hague: T.M.C. Asser Press, 2000. – p. 89.

According to the Code of Sport Ethics, 'Fair Game – Road to Victory', accepted 24 September 1992 by the Committee of Ministers of the Council of Europe, fair competition (a fair game) is defined as:

> Something that is more than playing by the rules. It incorporates the concepts of friendship, respect for others and always playing with the right spirit. Fair play is defined as a way of thinking, not just a way of behaving. It incorporates issues concerned with eliminating cheating, gamesmanship, doping, violence (both physical and verbal), the sexual harassment and abuse of children, young people and women, exploitation, unequal opportunities, excessive commercialization and corruption. Fair play is a positive concept. Sport is a social and cultural activity which, practised fairly, enriches society and friendship between nations. Sport is also recognized as an individual activity which, played fairly, offers the opportunity for self-knowledge, self-expression, fulfilment, personal achievement, skill acquisition, demonstration of ability, social interaction, enjoyment, good health and well-being. Sport promotes involvement and responsibility in society with its wide range of clubs and leaders working voluntarily. In addition, responsible involvement in some activities can help to promote sensitivity to the environment.

§2. Nature and Scope

48. The necessity of the legal regulation of sports relations has been caused primarily by the growing commercialization of professional sport since 1980. Since there is increasing capital for organizing and conducting sports competitions, professional sport has included economic aspects. Establishing labour relationships between highly paid sportspeople and sports clubs has led to the enrolment of lawyers acting as players' agents. Issues of intellectual property and the use of mass media are becoming more prolific, such as discussions over the rights to photographic images of sportspeople and sports competition translations.

49. EU law has played a considerable role in the development of sports jurisprudence. The well-known Bosman case in the mid-1990s significantly affected the existing system of transferring players in professional football. This case raised questions about the parity of legal acts of sports federations and the norms of national and international law, not only in EU countries but also in other states.

50. The LPCS was reviewed essentially with new wording in 2014, then in 2018. In 2014, the law increased in volume; its structure had been essentially changed. For the first time at a legislative level, the concepts of physical training and sport and the sportsperson had been accurately defined. The new law discussed the concept of a system of physical training and sport. For the regulation of sports relations, the new provisions established the concept of professional sport, forbade doping and enshrined a national regulation of the involvement of foreigners in sport.

51. The competitive character of sport defines the gravitation of sports law to the international arena. If the purpose of carrying out sports competitions is to reveal the fastest, strongest and highest, this can grow, and as a rule, it does to a planetary scale. The existence of the IOC and other international federations (IFs) is justified by the desire to hold international sports competitions. Accordingly, the legal acts of international sports federations have international characteristics. However, by their legal nature, they are obligatory only for the participants of competitive activities, unlike the international treaties concluded by the states.

52. The number of international conventions on sports regulations adopted by states is less than the regulations adopted by IFs. They concern, first, such important social problems as struggles against doping and violence at stadiums, when the intervention and coordinated efforts of states are especially necessary.

53. Belarus participates in the following conventions regulating sports or related to sports relations. Such international treaties are developed within the limits of the Council of Europe: the European convention on preventing violence and the hooligan behaviour of spectators during sporting events, particularly football matches, from 19 August 1985 (this has come into force in Russia and Ukraine), the Convention against doping, from 16 November 1989 (this has come into force in Russia, Ukraine and Belarus) and the Additional Report to the Convention against doping, from 12 September 2002 (this is signed by Ukraine). Belarus, as well as Russia and Ukraine, also participate in the United Nations Educational, Scientific and Cultural Organizations (UNESCO) International Convention against Doping in Sport, dated 19 October 2005.

54. A practical point is the legislative division of sport between professional and amateur. According to Article 55 of the LPCS, professional sport is the enterprise, labour and other activities, not forbidden by legislation, that are aimed at the achievement of high sports results and reception of income (compensation) for the organization of sports actions and (or) participation in them. Thus, the relations arising in professional sport between sportspeople, coaches, judges and other citizens conducting activities in the sphere of physical training and sport, and also the physical training and sports organizations and other organizations conducting activities in this sphere, are regulated by the Civil Code (CC) of Belarus, the LC, the LPCS and other legal acts.

55. Relations in the sphere of professional sport are regulated according to special legislation, along with administration by:

(1) Civil law norms (as the Belarus sports legislation directly orders).
(2) Norms of labour laws (as the Belarusian, Ukrainian and Russian sports legislation orders).

56. Application of the norms of civil, commercial and labour laws is justified by the specificity of professional sport as an activity connected with:

(1) the commercial activity in sport;
(2) professional sports relationships on the basis of labour laws (labour activity in sport);
(3) the reception of income from competitive activities, which is considered to be the only source of income.

57. Parties to labour relations in the field of sport include professional sportspeople and coaches as workers and sports clubs and organizations as employers. Relations of sports trade unions and club associations within the limits of social partnership (dialogue) have great value.

58. Tax law can contain special norms concerning the specificity of taxation for professional sportspeople and sports clubs.

59. The disputes arising from professional sports relationships can be resolved by orders generally established in the legislation and by orders provided by the legal acts of the sports organizations (the international and national federations), usually within the limits of disciplinary procedures, and also in special sports arbitration and mediation (national and international).

60. Professional sport is aimed at achieving high sports results or a set of records (Article 55(1) LPCS). One feature of higher achievement sport is its high level of socio-political importance. The state undertakes measures to support the subjects of professional sport. The Belarusian legislation lays down the principle of encouragement and promotes high-level sports development. The stated principle has a public-law character and is implemented through the establishment of a legal framework for the sports training of athletes and their participation in international competitions.

61. Amateur sport is a many-sided mass sport movement. It is that part of sport that is directed towards the physical training and physical development of citizens by means of carrying out organized and (or) independent employment and participation in sports actions and mass sports events. The norms of regulating the right to amateur sport have a public characteristic.

62. International sports relationships develop substantially within the limits of the Olympic and Paralympic movements. The Olympic movement includes the IOC, the Organizing Committees of the Olympic Games (OCOG), the National Olympic Committee (NOC), IFs, national associations, clubs, athletes, judges and all organizations and establishments recognized by the IOC. The Olympic movement is formed by all subjects who agree to be guided by the Olympic Charter[4] and

4. The Olympic Charter is the codification of fundamental principles, rules and the positions accepted by the International Olympic Committee. The Charter is the base document for the organization and management of the Olympic movement and defines the conduct of the Olympic Games. The operating edition of the Olympic Charter came into force on 17 Jul. 2020. The Charter text can be found on the official IOC website: http://www.olympic.org/Documents/olympic_charter_en.pdf.

recognize the competence of the IOC. According to the Olympic Charter, developed by Pierre de Coubertin, the goal of the Olympic movement is to contribute to building a peaceful and better world by educating youth through sport practised without discrimination of any kind and in the Olympic spirit, which requires mutual understanding with a spirit of friendship, solidarity and fair play.[5]

§3. Special Characteristics of National Sports Law

63. Belarusian sports law establishes the relationship of the state with sport as an element of international political propaganda. Belarus has tried to keep in line with Soviet sports policies, known on the world scene as high-level sports. In the country, there is a special Ministry of Sports and Tourism, and the heads of many national federations are appointed with the direct participation of the state.

64. The basic line of the Belarus sports law is the significant amount of imperative norms characterizing its administrative character. Its imperativeness is characterized by the presence of the following aspects:

(1) a state policy for the physical training and sports sphere;
(2) state regulations for the physical training and sports sphere;
(3) financing of physical training and sport by the state or by commercial institutes on the instruction of the state.

§4. Sources of Sports Law

65. Article 45 of the Constitution of Belarus establishes the right of citizens of Belarus to health protection, along with physical training and sports development. According to Article 32 of the Constitution, youths have a guaranteed right to spiritual, moral and physical development.

66. The basic source of sports law in Belarus is the LPCS, dated 4 January 2014, No. 125-Z (updated version: 9 January 2018, No. 92-Z).[6] The LPCS consists of ten chapters:

(1) General provisions.
(2) State policy in the sphere of physical training and sport.
(3) Organizing of physical training and sport.
(4) Physical training.
(5) General provisions on sport.
(6) High-level sport and professional sport.
(7) Training of sports reserves and high-level sportspeople:
(7-1) Volunteers and stewards and fans and fan associations.

5. Basic principles of the Olympic Charter.
6. The National Register of Legal Acts of Belarus, 15 Jan. 2014, No. 2/2123.

(8) Resource maintenance for physical training and sport.
(9) International cooperation in the sphere of physical training and sport.
(10) Final provisions.

67. The norms of the sports law regulations are contained in non-specialized statutory acts: the Criminal Code[7] (Article 253, Bribery of Participants and Organizers of Professional Sports Competitions or Commercial Entertainment Competitions) and the Law 'About the Provision of Pensions' (updated version: 29 December 2020)[8] (Article 49-2, 'Conditions for Appointment of Pensions to Sportspeople'). The LC,[9] in Chapter 26-1, establishes special procedures for employees who conduct their activity in the sphere of professional sport.

68. In the regulation of sports, the legal acts of the Ministry of Sports and Tourism of Belarus play an important role. The most significant are the following sections of the Resolution: No. 11, dated 28 December 2004 (updated version: 15 May 2018) 'On the Statement of Positions for Specialized Sports Establishments';[10] No. 16, dated 2 July 2014 (updated version: 29 September 2020) 'On Approval of the Regulations for State Sports Complexes of the Republic of Belarus';[11] No. 73/102, dated 28 November 2014 (updated version: 4 July 2019) 'Some Questions of Contract with the Sportspeople-Instructors and Coaches of the National Teams of the Republic of Belarus by Type of Sport';[12] No. 22, dated 11 July 2014 (updated version: 26 June 2017) 'On Approval of the Anti-Doping Rules of the Republic of Belarus';[13] No. 3, dated 16 February 2007 (updated version: 17 June 2020) 'On the Instruction Statement about the Admission Order to Pedagogical Activity in the Physical Training and Sports Sphere and an Order of Passage by Special Preparation for the Admission to Employment in Pedagogical Activity in the Physical Training and Sports Sphere';[14] No. 64, dated 8 October 2014 (updated version: 15 January 2019) 'On the Rules on Uniform Sport Classification of Belarus';[15] No. 62, dated 6 October 2014 'On the Rules of Sports Judges';[16] No. 27, dated 10 June 2010 (updated version: 11 April 2018) 'On the Rules of Domestic Review-Competitions',[17] No. 19, dated 26 February 2010 (updated version: 22 August 2018) 'On the Instructions for Assigning Qualifying Categories to Coaches-Teachers of Sport and Other Categories of Employees in the Physical Training and Sports Sphere';[18] No. 10, dated 30 April 2015 (updated version: 15 April 2021) 'On an Establishment of Monetary Norms of Expenses for Food for Pupils of High Schools

7. The Criminal Code of Republic of Belarus dated 9 Jul. 1999 No. 275-Z (in version dated 26 May 2021) //http://pravo.by/document/?guid=3871&p0=hk9900275.
8. Viedamasci Viarchoŭnaha Savieta Respubliki Belarus', 15 Jun. 1992, No. 17, Art. 275.
9. http://etalonline.by/PrintText.aspx?regnum=HK9900296.
10. The National Register of Legal Acts of Belarus, 9 Feb. 2005, No. 21, 8/12042.
11. The National Register of Legal Acts of Belarus, 29 Aug. 2014, No. 8/29060.
12. The National Register of Legal Acts of Belarus, 31 Dec. 2014, No. 8/29460.
13. The National Register of Legal Certificates of Belarus, 18 Nov. 2014, No. 8/29292.
14. The National Register of Legal Acts of Belarus, 2 Apr. 2007, No. 79, 8/15999.
15. The National Register of Legal Acts of Belarus, 5 Dec. 2014, No. 8/29334.
16. The National Register of Legal Acts of Belarus, 5 Dec. 2014, No. 8/29331.
17. The National Register of Legal Acts of Belarus, 13 Jul. 2010, No. 162, 8/22507.
18. The National Register of Legal Acts of Belarus, 21 Jun. 2010, No. 146, 8/22428.

– Schools for Olympic Reserves';[19] No. 30, dated 28 September 2020 'On the Provision of Sports Equipment';[20] No. 40, dated 21 July 2014 (updated version: 8 December 2016) 'On the Rules for Schools of Olympic Reserves'[21] and others.

69. Belarus participates in the following international conventions concerning sport:

(1) The UN 'International Convention against Apartheid in Sports' (adopted in New York on 10 December 1985).[22]
(2) The Convention of the Council of Europe No. 135 – the 'Anti-Doping Convention' (signed in Strasbourg on 16 November 1989).[23]
(3) The Convention of the Council of Europe No. 120 – 'The European Convention on Spectator Violence and Misbehaviour at Sports Events and in particular Football Matches' (signed in Strasbourg on 19 August 1985).
(4) The UNESCO 'International Convention against Doping in Sport' (signed in Paris on 19 October 2005).[24]

70. The conventions with an indirect relation to sport, regulating the right to play sport and the principle of 'sport for all' are:

(a) The UN 'Convention on the Elimination of All Forms of Discrimination against Women' (signed in New York on 18 December 1979).

71. Cooperation agreements in the field of sport and tourism include:

(a) The agreement between the Ministry of Sports and Tourism of Belarus and the Ministry of Culture, Sport and Tourism of the Socialist Republic of Vietnam 'On Cooperation in the Field of Sport and Tourism' (concluded in Hanoi on 7 April 2008).[25]
(b) The Cooperation Agreement in the field of physical training and sport between the participants of the Commonwealth of Independent States and the 'Position on the Council for Physical Training and Sport of the Participants of the Cooperation Agreement in the Field of Physical Training and Sport within the Commonwealth of Independent States') (concluded in Yalta on 25 May 2007).[26]

19. The National Register of Legal Acts of Belarus, 11 Jun. 2015, No. 8/29983.
20. The National Register of Legal Acts of Belarus, 13 Oct. 2020, No. 8/35912.
21. The National Register of Legal Acts of Belarus, 3 Sep. 2014, No. 8/29079.
22. The Code of Laws of the BSSR, decrees of the Presidium of the Supreme Council of the BSSR, resolutions of the Council of Ministers of the BSSR, 1987, No. 15, Art. 178.
23. The National Register of Legal Acts of Belarus, 6 Feb. 2006, No. 20, 2/1180.
24. The National Register of Legal Acts of Belarus, 28 Jul. 2008, No. 175, 2/1498.
25. The National Register of Legal Acts of Belarus, 8 May 2008, No. 108, 3/2118.
26. The National Register of Legal Acts of Belarus, 10 Sep. 2008, No. 213, 3/2150.

(c) The agreement between the Ministry of Sports and Tourism of Belarus and the Ministry of Youth and Sport for the Republic of Moldova 'On Cooperation in the Field of Physical Training and Sport' (concluded in Baku on 21 September 2010).[27]
(d) The agreement between the Government of Belarus and the Government of Turkmenistan 'On Cooperation in the Field of Sport and Tourism' (concluded in Ashgabat on 18 June 2009).[28]
(e) The agreement between the Ministry of Sports and Tourism of Belarus and the Ministry of Culture, Information and Sport for the Republic of Kazakhstan 'On Cooperation in the Field of Physical Training and Sport' (concluded in Astana on 18 May 2005).[29]
(f) The agreement between the Ministry of Sports and Tourism of Belarus and the Ministry of Youth and Sport Affairs for the Republic of India 'On Cooperation in the Field of Physical Training and Sport' (concluded in Minsk on 17 September 2009).[30]
(g) The agreement between the Government of Belarus and the Government of the Democratic Socialist Republic of Sri Lanka 'On Cooperation in the Field of Tourism' (concluded in Minsk on 26 August 2013).

72. Belarus also joined the expanded partial agreement on sports founded by the resolution of the Committee of Ministers of the Council of Europe, CM/Res (2007), of 11 May 2007.[31]

27. Not published officially.
28. The National Register of Legal Acts of Belarus, 26 May 2010, No. 123, 3/2528.
29. The National Register of Legal Acts of Belarus, 18 Dec. 2009, No. 301, 3/2361.
30. The National Register of Legal Acts of Belarus, 13 Oct. 2009, No. 240, 3/2331.
31. Edict of the President of Republic of Belarus of 24 Nov. 2008, No. 638 'On accession of the Republic of Belarus to the Enlarged Partial Agreement on Sport // The National Register of Legal Acts of Belarus, 1 Dec. 2008, No. 287, 1/10249.

Chapter 2. Public Regulations

§1. Systems of Physical Training and Sport: Freedom of Association

73. According to Article 8 of the LPCS, physical training and sports systems in Belarus include:

(1) The Ministry of Sports and Tourism of Belarus, other republican bodies of state administration, institutions of local government and other state bodies (organizations) operating in the sphere of physical training and sport according to the competence of the administration.
(2) Physical training and sports organizations.
(3) Sportspeople and other individuals engaged in physical training and sport and their associations, including clubs for physical training and sport.
(4) Sports judges, coaches, sporting agents and other specialists in the sphere of physical training and sport and their associations.
(5) Volunteers, stewards, sponsors and advertisers operating in the field of physical training and sport.
(6) Fans and fan associations.
(7) Educational institutions, scientific organizations and health care organizations operating in the field of physical training and sport.
(8) Other persons operating in the field of physical training and sport.

In Belarus, commercial and non-commercial organizations for physical training and sport can be created (Article 16 LPCS). Organizations for physical training and sport are legal entities, which aim to:

(1) develop physical training and (or) sport; prepare sports reserves and (or) high-level sportspeople; improve sports and (or) engage in mass sport work;
(2) conduct sports actions and (or) participate in them, including preparing sportspeople (teams) and representing sportspeople (teams) on their own behalf at sports competitions;
(3) maintain a system of physical training and sport;
(4) support the training of sportspeople (teams) scientifically and medically;
(5) prevent and fight against doping in sport – doping control.

According to Article 16(3) of the LPCS, the organizations of physical training and sport are:

(1) The National Olympic Committee of the Republic of Belarus.
(2) The PC of Belarus and organizations heading the Deaflympics movement of Belarus and the Special Olympic movement of Belarus.
(3) The National Anti-Doping Agency.
(4) Sports federations (unions, associations) by type of sport.
(5) Republican state and public associations for the development of technology, aviation and military applications and service.

(6) Specialized educational sports establishments, clubs by type of sport.
(7) Healthcare and sports centres (training centres, centres for sport and recreation activities, centres of physical care activity) and physical clubs.
(8) Training centres for the physical education of the population, centres for physical education and sport for pupils and students.
(9) Sports camps (in case of the registration as a legal entity).
(10) Other organizations of physical training and sport.

74. Physical training and sports organizations are created, reorganized and liquidated according to the CC of Belarus and other legal acts, considering the requirements provided by the LPCS (Article 17). Creation, reorganization and liquidation of state organizations of physical training and sport are carried out in coordination with the Ministry of Sports and Tourism unless otherwise defined by legislative acts.

75. The NOC is the public organization recognized by the IOC. The NOC of Belarus heads the Olympic movement of Belarus and works with the Ministry of Sports and Tourism to develop and implement a uniform state policy for the development of higher-level sport. It is guided in its activity by the legislation of Belarus, the Olympic Charter, other decisions of the IOC and the NOC Charter of the IOC (Article 18 LPCS).

76. According to Article 19 of the LPCS, the Paralympic Committee (PC) of Belarus is the public organization recognized by the International Paralympic Committee. The PC of Belarus heads the Paralympic movement of Belarus and works with the Ministry of Sports and Tourism, the Ministry of Labour and Social Protection, the Ministry of Health, the Ministry of Education and public disability associations to develop and implement a uniform state policy for the development of physical training and sports among people with a disability, including children with special developmental needs. It is guided in its activity by the legislation of Belarus, the Charter of the International Paralympic Committee and the Paralympic Charter.

77. Article 21 of the LPCS establishes the concept of federations by type of sport. According to this, a federation (union, association) is a non-commercial organization created in the form of a public association or union with a view of developing a type/s of sport in Belarus and conducting relevant sports competitions.

78. Sports federations work with the Ministry of Sports and Tourism of Belarus, the NOC of Belarus and the PC of Belarus to develop and implement a uniform state policy for the development of a type/s of sports and conduct other activities according to the LPCS and other legal acts.

A sports federation that is a member of an international sports association can be accredited as a national sports federation by the Ministry of Sports and Tourism, according to an order established by the Resolution of the Ministry of Sports and Tourism dated 17 July 2014, No. 36 (updated version: 27 July 2018 No. 50).[32]

32. The National Register of Legal Acts of Belarus, 28 Oct. 2014, No. 8/29220.

79. The status of a national sports federation cannot be appointed to more than one sports organization for each type of sport. Decisions of the Ministry of Sports and Tourism about assigning the status of national federation can be appealed according to an order established by the legislation.

80. To obtain the status of national federation, the organization must provide the Ministry of Sports and Tourism with the following documents:

(1) a statement listing the name and federation location;
(2) the certificate for the state registration of the federation;
(3) a copy of the document with an assured translation into Russian or Belarusian, when due hereunder, confirming federation membership of an international sport association;
(4) the rules for conducting competitions of the type(s) of sport it represents;
(5) the programme of development of the sport represented by the federation, in the current or next Olympic cycle.

81. The decision to assign an organization the status of national federation is made by the Ministry of Sports and Tourism within one month from the date of receipt of the required documents. Assignment of the status of national federation is proven true by the certificate. The national federation is entered into the register kept by the Ministry of Sports and Tourism.

82. The certificate is signed by the Minister of Sports and Tourism or an assistant authorized by him. The period of certificate validity is four or eight years. An organization admitted as a national federation is given a certificate. The duration of the certificate's validity corresponds to the duration of the federation's admission to the register of national federations. The certificate specifies:

(1) the name of the body that has granted the certificate;
(2) the registration number of the certificate and the date of its delivery;
(3) the number and date of the decision to assign the organization the status of national federation;
(4) the period of validity;
(5) the data on the federation (the name and location, the name of the registering body, the number and date of the certificate in the state register);
(6) the sport type/s for which the status of national federation is appropriated.

83. Organizations' applications for the status of national federation can be rejected when:

(1) there is no legal basis for conducting the administrative procedure for the admission of the federation;
(2) state organs are provided with documents and (or) information that is inconsistent with the legislation, including false, falsified or invalid documents.

84. An organization can be deprived by the Ministry of Sports and Tourism of the status of national federation on the following basis:

(1) non-compliance with the terms of the contract on the development of the specified type of sport;
(2) secession of the federation from the international sports organization;
(3) federation liquidation;
(4) failure of the organization to engage in activity directed towards the realization of its authorized purposes and problems for more than six months;
(5) infringement of the legislation of Belarus by the organization;
(6) expiry of the duration of admission to the register of national federations.

85. Article 23 of the LPCS regulates the concept of specialized sports schools, which are non-commercial specialized sports organizations aimed at preparing sports reserves and (or) high-level sportspeople. Types of specialized sports establishments include:

(1) Child–youth sports schools
(2) Child–youth sports-technical schools
(3) Specialized child–youth schools for Olympic reserves
(4) Specialized sports-technical schools
(5) Centres for Olympic reserves
(6) Centres for Olympic preparation.

86. Specialized sports schools can conduct activities after state accreditation by the Ministry of Sports and Tourism (the Resolution of by the Ministry of Sports and Tourism dated 21 October 2014, No. 66).[33] The state accreditation of specialized sports establishment includes the procedure for recognizing the status as a specialized sports establishment of the corresponding type and confirming the presence in the establishment of resource maintenance that meets the requirements for the corresponding type of specialized sports school and the established legislation.

87. Specialized sports schools operate on the basis of charters developed according to general provisions for the specialized sports establishments of the appropriate type, as confirmed by the Ministry of Sports and Tourism. Preparation in specialized sports schools is conducted on the basis of programmes confirmed by the Ministry of Sports and Tourism.

88. With a view of maintaining state control over the quality of preparation in specialized sports schools, their certification is conducted as specified in the order confirmed by the Ministry of Sports and Tourism of Belarus. The state certification of specialized sports establishments confirms the maintenance and quality of preparation in specialized sports establishments by type of sport. Due to state certification, specialized sports establishments can be transformed into specialized sports

33. The National Register of Legal Acts of Belarus, 1 Dec. 2014, No. 8/29318.

establishments of other types. If the specialized sports establishment has not received state certification, the process to obtain state certification should be repeated in a year. In the case of non-passing of repeated attempts to obtain state certifications, the specialized sports establishment loses its status.

89. The state certification for child–youth sports schools for general physical preparation, child–youth sports schools, child–youth sports-technical schools, specialized child–youth schools for Olympic reserves and specialized sports-technical schools is issued by local executive and administrative bodies. The state certification for centres for Olympic reserves and centres for Olympic preparation is issued by the Ministry of Sports and Tourism.

90. Sports clubs are organizations aimed at preparing sportspeople (teams) and representing sportspeople (teams) at sports competitions based on the type of sport (Article 24 LPCS).

91. A sports centre (a complex) is an organization with the property, economic ability or operational administration of sports facilities that provides these constructs to citizens and organizations to conduct sporting activities or to render sport-improving services (Article 25 LPCS).

§2. Governmental Conditions and Permits

92. According to Article 9 of the LPCS, the state policy in the sphere of physical training and sport focuses on sports development and support and is based on the following principles:

(1) democracy and the elimination of discrimination and violence in the sphere of physical culture and sport;
(2) accessibility, voluntariness and continuity of physical culture and sport;
(3) interaction between physical culture and sport;
(4) the combination of state and social regulations and control in the sphere of physical culture and sport;
(5) respect for and compliance with international obligations in the sphere of physical culture and sport.

93. Support for physical training and sport is conducted according to state programmes for the development of physical training and sport (Article 10 LPCS). These government programmes are approved by the Ministry of Sports and Tourism. Belarus currently has a state programme established by the Resolution of the Council of Ministers of the Republic of Belarus of 29 January 2021 'On the State

Programme "Physical Culture and Sport" for 2021–2025'.[34] This resolution incorporates the main goals and objectives of the State programme, the issues of financial security, the assessment of major risks and their management, and the methodology for evaluating the effectiveness of the State programme. State regulation for the physical training and sports sphere (Article 11 LPCS) is carried out by the President of Belarus, the Parliament of Belarus, the Council of Ministers of Belarus, the Ministry of Sports and Tourism of Belarus, local councils of deputies, executive and administrative bodies and other state bodies within their powers, according to the legislation.

94. The President of Belarus defines a uniform state policy for physical training and sport. The Council of Ministers of Belarus provides specifications for carrying out this uniform state policy. The Ministry of Sports and Tourism carries out the state policy and activities of coordination in the sphere of physical training and sport for other republican state bodies. Local councils of deputies and the executive and administrative bodies solve questions in the sphere of physical training and sport within their competence.

95. Physical training and sport financing are conducted at the expense of republican and local budgetary funds for the physical training and sports organizations and other organizations that have been not forbidden by the legislation (Article 65 LPCS).

96. According to Article 69 of the LPCS, pedagogical activity in the sphere of physical training and sport can be carried out by citizens with a special or higher education in the sphere of physical training and sport, as well as citizens admitted to such activity in an order confirmed by the Ministry of Sports and Tourism of Belarus. Such citizens who, five or more years after obtaining a diploma (admission to pedagogical activity in the physical training and sports sphere), have not carried out pedagogical activity in physical training and sport or, having stopped such activity during this term, have not renewed it can be readmitted to pedagogical activity in the sphere of physical training and sport after completing special preparations.

97. Preparation, improvement of professional skills and retraining of personnel in physical training and sport are carried out in educational institutions according to the legislation (Article 68 LPCS).

§3. Fundamental Rights and Obligations

98. Article 4 of the LPCS 'The Right to Engage in Physical Training and Sport' declares that:

(1) each citizen of Belarus has the right to engage in physical training and sport;

---

34. The National Register of Legal Acts of Belarus, 4 Feb. 2021, No. 5/48742.

(2) the right of the citizens of Belarus to engage in physical training and sport is provided by the state via the creation of necessary conditions for the enjoyment of this right and the carrying out of state policy in the sphere of physical training and sport.

99. According to Article 4 of the LPCS, foreign citizens and persons without citizenship within the territory of the Republic of Belarus enjoy the rights in the sphere of physical culture and sport on an equal basis with citizens of the Republic of Belarus, unless otherwise defined by the Constitution of the Republic.

§4. Physical Culture

100. Article 29 of the LPCS regulates the concept of 'the state sport-improving structure of the Republic of Belarus'. The state sport-improving structure of Belarus is a set of programmes and specifications that are the basis for the physical training of the citizens of Belarus, with due consideration of sex, age and other factors. The state sport-improving structure of Belarus defines the purposes and problems of physical training of citizens and the level of their physical readiness. It consists of three programmes: sport and fitness, motivation, and sport promotion. The state sport-improving structure of Belarus is affirmed by the Government or the state body authorized by it.

101. The formation of establishments according to legislation, on the basis of charters, defines the means of physical education and the methods of conducting studies on the basis of typical plans and programmes for physical training. Those establishments also conduct additional sport-improving and mass sport work, including the work of physical training and sports organizations (Article 32 LPCS).

102. In the establishments providing pre-school education, physical training is obligatory and is carried out in the course of various types of children's activities, according to plans and programmes for physical training and sanitary and hygiene requirements (Article 32(3) LPCS).

103. The establishments providing pre-school education can focus on physical training according to the legislation on their formation (Article 32(4) LPCS).

104. Physical training in establishments providing pre-school education, general level education, professional-technical education and average vocational education is carried out in the form of lessons on physical culture, learning sessions on the discipline of physical culture and health, sport-improving and mass sport participation events and in other forms in accordance with the legislation of Belarus (Article 32(4) LPCS).

105. In accordance with Article 32(5) of the LPCS, obligatory lessons on physical training within the discipline of physical culture and health ('Adaptive Physical Culture'), except as provided for in paragraph 6 of this Article, shall be conducted during the entire period of study in accordance with the teaching and corresponding documentation of the educational programme:

(1) at least two hours of training in a school week within general education, vocational education at the level of general education and professional-technical and general education;
(2) at least three teaching hours in a school week within professional-technical and general education, except in cases specified in the second part of this paragraph.

106. Physical training in establishments providing full-time higher education at the level of an undergraduate degree is obligatory during all periods of education and is conducted no less than four hours per week for the first and second courses and no less than two hours per week for the third course, in the form of studies of physical training, according to the curricula and programmes on physical training.

107. When conducting additional sport-improving and mass sport work in the establishments providing general average, professional, average special and higher education, circles, groups and organizations by sport types are to be developed.

108. Pupils and students undertake annual medical examinations in public health service organizations, the results of which are distributed in the basic, preparatory and special medical groups and groups of medical physical training.

109. Pupils and students with weakened health are engaged in special medical groups and groups taking part in medical physical training on the basis of specially developed programmes for physical training.

110. According to Article 30 of the LPCS 'Physical Training at the Workplace', the realizations by workers of the right to physical training include:

(1) carrying out sport improving and mass sport work with workers and members of their families;
(2) building and maintenance of sports constructions;
(3) creating structural division (introduction of expert positions) and conducting activities with a focus on physical training and sport development;
(4) providing assistance to associations of workers in physical training collectives;
(5) realization of other activities not forbidden by legislation and promoting the realization by workers of the right to physical training in the workplace.

111. Article 31 of the LPCS regulates sports activities at the place of residence. Local executive and administrative bodies will provide conditions for the physical training of citizens at the place of residence. To maintain the right of citizens to physical training at the place of residence, local executive and administrative bodies:

(1) independently or together with physical training and sports organizations and other organizations conducting activities in the sphere of physical training and sport carry out sport-improving and mass sport work with citizens at the place of residence;
(2) create and finance sports centres with a wide set of sport-improving services;
(3) establish procedures for the provision of health and sport services with partial or full payment of their costs in organizations of public utility ownership located in the relevant territory;
(4) in an order established by the legislation, allocate necessary premises, provide sport constructions to organizations of physical training and sport for carrying out sport-improving and mass sport work and provide other assistance to physical training and sports organizations;
(5) organize the work of affinity groups, sectioned by sport type;
(6) provide persons with disabilities with the necessary conditions for free access and use of sports facilities and provide special sports equipment;
(7) together with the parties concerned, create conditions for the sport training in recreational areas;
(8) carry out, according to their competence, other activities promoting the realization by citizens of the right to physical training.

112. Article 33 of the LPCS establishes that the physical preparation of members of the military, persons commanding and part of the ordinary structure of law-enforcement bodies, bodies of financial investigations of the Committee of the State Control of Belarus, bodies and divisions on extreme situations, public prosecution workers and officials of customs bodies is one of the basic subjects of fighting and (or) vocational training and an important and integral part of their education. The organization and financing of their physical preparation are carried out according to the legislation, including republican state-public associations.

113. Physical preparation of citizens for military service is carried out in the establishments providing general, professional and average vocational education, according to curricula and educational standards.

114. Citizens who are subject to call up for military service can be engaged in military-applied types of sport in republican state-public associations, public associations, schools, clubs and sections by type of sport.

115. The organization of sport-improving and mass sport work with the handicapped, including children with abnormal psychophysical development, is carried out by the Ministry of Education of Belarus, the Ministry of Health of Belarus, the Ministry of Sports and Tourism of Belarus, the Ministry of Labour and Social Protection of Belarus, local executive and administrative bodies and other state bodies according to their competence.

116. Specified establishments, as well as state bodies, conduct sport-improving and mass sport work with the handicapped together with the PC of Belarus.

§5. General Rules on Sport

117. With a view of preparing sports reserves and (or) high-level sportspeople, the system of specialized sports school is financed at the expense of the republican and (or) local budgetary funds, as well as other sources of financing that are not forbidden by legislation (Article 60 LPCS).

118. The right to free preparation in specialized sports schools financed at the expense of republican and (or) local budgetary funds is granted to the citizens of Belarus, as well as foreign citizens and persons without citizenship who have passed competitive selection and do not have contraindications for employment by the selected type of sport (Article 60(2) LPCS).

119. Estimated admission figures (acquisition plans) for pupils without payment for preparation in specialized sports schools, financed at the expense of the republican budgetary funds, is defined by the Ministry of Sports and Tourism of Belarus and, in the establishments financed at the expense of local budgetary funds, by local executive and administrative bodies (Article 60(3) LPCS).

120. Specialized educational and sports schools and child and youth sports schools (specialized child and youth schools for Olympic reserves) included in the structure of sports clubs in the form of separate structural units, financed by republican and (or) local budgets, in excess of control figures for admission (acquisition plans), without a fee, can receive for sports training those who have not passed the competitive selection and bear medical contraindications to engage in selected sports for a fee, in compliance with the rules and regulations of the organization of the training process (Article 60(4) LPCS).

121. The specialized sports schools funded at the expense of other sources not forbidden by legislation can define, in coordination with the proprietor, estimated reception figures (acquisition plans) without payment for preparation (Article 60(5) LPCS).

122. Orders for the reception, transfer, deduction and restoration of sportspeople is established by the Ministry of Sports and Tourism (Article 60(7) LPCS).

123. The payment for preparation is established by the head of a specialized sports establishment at a rate of economically proven expenses, in coordination with the legislation. Under the decision of the head of a specialized sports establishment, the size of a tuition fee can be differentiated depending on the level of achievement in the sport (Article 60(8) LPCS).

124. Uniform Sport Classification of Belarus: a set of norms and requirements necessary for assigning sports categories and ranks, as well as conditions and an order of their assignment. The order and conditions for awarding, depriving and restoring sports categories and ranks are established in the Regulations on Uniform Sport Classification of the Republic of Belarus (Article 40 LPCS).

125. National teams of Belarus by sport type: collectives of sportspeople, coaches and other experts formed to prepare for international sports competitions and participation in them as symbols of Belarus (Article 1 LPCS).

126. The national sports teams of Belarus are formed by the Ministry of Sports and Tourism of Belarus taking into account tendencies of the development of sport and the results of sportspeople after representing national federations (unions, associations) by type of sport and other organizations according to the legislation (Article 54(1) LPCS).

127. The 'recognized' national sports teams of Belarus are formed within the number established by the Government of Belarus; the other national teams of Belarus are formed within the number established by the Ministry of Sports and Tourism (Article 54(2) LPCS).

128. Members of the national sports teams of Belarus not meeting established specifications and (or) regularly breaking duties can be removed from national teams according to the procedure established by the Ministry of Sports and Tourism (Article 54(3) LPCS).

129. The orders for forming the national sports teams of Belarus and dismissal from the national sports teams of Belarus are established by the Ministry of Sports and Tourism (Article 54(4) LPCS).

130. Material, medical, methodological and (or) other support of the national teams of Belarus and financing of their preparation for and participation in international sports actions are conducted at the expense of the republican budgetary funds and from the donations of citizens, legal bodies and other sources not forbidden by the legislation (Article 54(5) LPCS).

§6. Status of Sports Federations

131. In Belarus, sport development is carried out through the close interaction of state and public organizations. According to Article 9 of the LPCS, the interaction of state bodies with the NOC of Belarus, the PC of Belarus, national federations (unions, associations) and other organizations of physical training and sport is one of the state's policy principles on physical training and sport.

132. Article 16 of the LPCS states that in Belarus, commercial and noncommercial organizations of physical training and sport (sports organizations) can be created and an exhaustive list of employment types is provided, which should be specified in the constituent documents of the organizations as an activity subject to admitting the organization (legal body).

133. Article 17 of the LPCS refers to questions on the creation, reorganization and liquidation of sports organizations within the CC and other legal acts, considering the requirements provided by paragraph 2 of this Article.

134. Article 21 of the LPCS defines a sports federation. A federation (union, association) is a non-commercial organization created in the form of a public association or union with a focus on the development of sport in Belarus; it is the organization carrying out sports competitions.

135. The concrete duties of a sports federation in the LPCS include:

(1) taking measures aimed at the development of the type/s of sports;
(2) protecting the rights and interests of professional sports actors;
(3) contributing to the prevention of doping in the sports sphere;
(4) counteracting all forms of discrimination and violence in sport;
(5) participating in medical and (or) other support of sportspeople and coaches;
(6) participating in the development of infrastructure and material and technical bases for the relevant type/s of sports;
(7) performing other duties in accordance with this Law, other legislative acts and their statutes (Article 21).

136. Summarizing all positions of the LPCS, it is possible to allocate the following fundamental norms of sports federations:

(1) to organize official championships and draws of Belarus by type of sport, according to their competence (Article 42);
(2) to represent the interests of Belarus in international sports organizations through the sporting and other actions carried out by international sports organizations (Article 73);
(3) To represent the Ministry of Sports and Tourism of Belarus in forming national sports teams (Article 54);
(4) to remove members of national teams by type of sport who have not met the established specifications and (or) regularly break the rules (Article 54);
(5) to participate in the material support of the national sports teams of Belarus by financing their preparation for international sports actions and participating in them (Article 54).

137. It is possible to establish in various legal acts the following rights of sports federations:[35]

(1) to organize, including on a reward basis, sports competitions, to sell tickets and broadcasting rights and to use the received means for performance of the authorized purposes and problems;

35. Kamenkov V.S. 'Pravovoi status sportivnoifederatcii v Respublike Belarus' // Consultant Plus [Electronic legal database].

(2) to present documents of assignment of members of national sports teams and coaches of all categories and sport teams employed during the current year, including the minimum tariff category or the tariff category corresponding to the results achieved during the past year;[36]
(3) to put forward nominees for the special award of the President of Belarus, the 'Belarusian Sports Olympus';
(4) to be a part of the faculty council of youth sports schools;[37]
(5) to be a part of the commission on the state certification of specialized sports establishments;[38]
(6) to deprive sportspeople and coaches of nominal grants of the President of Belarus (reduction of their size) for infringement of a sporting rule or labour discipline;[39]
(7) to assign sports referees to international categories;
(8) to confirm curriculums of seminars on the special preparation of sports referees;
(9) to apply disciplinary measures to judges of sports, including the prevention, discharge and decrease or deprivation of a sports referee's category for default or inadequate performance of duties.[40]

138. Article 20 of the law on public associations gives a very generous list of the rights of sports federations:

(1) to carry out activities aimed at achieving the authorized purpose;
(2) to freely receive and extend information concerning their activity;
(3) to use public funds according to an order established by the legislation;
(4) to establish their own mass media and to publish in accordance with an order established by the legislation;

36. Establishing Criteria in Assessing Performance of Athletes and Trainers of all Categories of National Sports Teams of the Armed Forces of the Republic of Belarus and Sports Teams in Team Sports among the Civilian Personnel of the Armed Forces of the Republic of Belarus for determining Tariff Categories: Regulation of Ministry of Defence of republic of Belarus, 31 Oct. 2006, No. 50 // The National Register of Legal Acts of Belarus. – 2006. – No. 207. – 8/15463.
37. On Approval of Provisions on Specialized Training and Sports Facilities: the Regulation of the Ministry of Sports and Tourism of the Republic of Belarus, 28 Dec. 2004, No. 11 (in the version dated 15 May 2018) // The National Register of Legal Acts of Belarus. – 2005, No. 21. 8/12042.
38. On some issues of state accreditation and state certification of organizations for the right to carry out activities to prepare a sports reserve and (or) high-class athletes: the decision of the Ministry of Sports and Tourism of the Republic of Belarus, 21 Oct. 2014 No. 66 // The National Register of Legal Acts of Belarus, 1 Dec. 2014, No. 8/29318.
39. Presidential Edict of 15 Apr. 2013, No. 190 'On Measures to Encourage Achievement of High Sports Results' (with the 'Regulations on the Appointment and Payment of Stipends of the President of the Republic of Belarus in the Sphere of Physical Culture and Sports', 'Regulations on the Procedure for Issuing Awards, Prizes, Monetary or In-kind Payments to Athletes and Coaches') (in the version dated 2 Oct. 2014, No. 464) // The National Legal Internet Portal of the Republic of Belarus, 18 Apr. 2013, 1/14217.
40. *See* Resolution of the Ministry of Sports and Tourism of the Republic of Belarus of 6 Oct. 2014, No. 62 'On Approval of the Rules on Sports Referees' (The National Register of Legal Acts of Belarus, 2014. 8/29331).

(5) to protect the rights and legitimate interests and represent the legitimate interests of members of state bodies and other organizations;
(6) to participate in elections in accordance with an order established by the legislation;
(7) to maintain relations with other public associations and unions;
(8) to create unions;
(9) to carry out, when due hereunder, commercial activity only so far as it is necessary for their authorized purposes, for the sake of which they are created, and corresponds to these purposes and is included in the activity of a public association. Such activity can be carried out by a public association only by means of forming commercial organizations and (or) participating in them unless otherwise provided for by legislative acts;
(10) to have other rights provided by the law for public associations and other acts.

139. The order of assigning the status of national federation is established in the Resolution of the Ministry of Sports and Tourism of Belarus dated 17 July 2014, No. 36, 'On Rules of Maintenance of the Register of Sports Federations (Unions, Associations) by the Type of Sport' (updated version: 27 July 2018, No. 50).[41] The so-called national federations can count on more attention and assistance from the state.

§7. Status of Sports Clubs

140. A sports club is defined in the LPCS as an organization conducting activities to prepare sportspeople (teams) and to represent sportspeople (teams) on its own behalf at sports competitions, by type of sport.[42]

141. A sports club's essential rights and duties can be met in a set of legal acts. For example, Article 44 of the Budgetary Code of Belarus[43] sets the financing of expenses for sports clubs and sport-related organizations. Financing is sourced:

(1) from regional budgets – support of sports clubs and other organizations that provide services in the field of physical culture and sport (Article 45 of the Budgetary Code of the Republic of Belarus);
(2) from budgets of a base level – support of sports clubs (Article 46 of the Budgetary Code of the Republic of Belarus);
(3) from the budget of Minsk – support of sports clubs and other organizations that provide services in the field of physical culture and sport (Article 47 of the Budgetary Code of the Republic of Belarus).

41. The National Register of Legal Acts of Belarus, 28 Oct. 2014, No. 8/29220.
42. *See also* Kamenkov V.S. Pravovoe polozhenie sportivnogo cluba / V.S.Kamenkov // Sportivnoe pravo v Respublike Belarus: sb. st. / sost.: red. zhurn. 'Promyshlenno-torgovoe pravo'. – Minsk: red. zhurn. 'Promyshlenno-torgovoe pravo', 2011. – 288 P. – P. 14 – 15.
43. Budgetary Code of the Republic of Belarus of 16 Jul. 2008, No. 412-Z // The National Register of Legal Acts of Belarus, 2008, No. 183, 2/1509.

142. In the Decree of the President of Belarus dated 29 March 2012, No. 150, 'On Some Questions of Rent and Gratuitous Use of Property' (updated version: 16 September 2019, No. 343),[44] sports clubs, health schools, sports sections and groups, centres for sport-improving work and child–youth sports schools are included in the list of legal bodies and individual businesses where real estate owned by the state is given for gratuitous use.

143. In many instructions of the Ministry of Sports and Tourism, a sports club should be established mostly as a legal body or branch.[45] First, the clubs created by state authorities must create branch sports clubs according to the legislation of Belarus in any organizational-legal form, for increasing the efficiency of sport-improving and mass sport work in organizations of corresponding branches.[46] Second, sports clubs are created according to the legislation of Belarus within organizations in any form, for increasing the efficiency of sport in the organization. Sports clubs should have the status of a legal person. A 'Legal body is the organization which has in the property rights, economic conducting or an operational administration the isolated property, bears independent responsibility under the obligations, can get and carry out on its own behalf the property and personal non-property rights, fulfil duties, to be the claimant and the respondent in the court, passed when due hereunder the state registration as the legal person or recognized as that act' (Article 44 CC). 'The legal body has the name containing information on its organizational-legal form' (Article 50 CC). If not given the status of a legal person, it will be impossible for sports clubs to obtain the rights listed above to receive material and other maintenance from the state.

144. In relation to the creation, reorganization and liquidation of organizations of physical training and sport, the LPCS refers to the CC (Article 17). Sports clubs can be commercial and non-commercial legal bodies. That the sports club is among a physical training and sports organization is directly specified in Article 16 of the LPCS; the subject activities of such legal bodies are also designated in the named rule of law.

---

44. Presidential Edict of 29 Mar. 2012, No. 150 'On Some Issues of Rent and Gratuitous Use of Property' (with the 'Regulations for the rental of permanent structures (buildings), isolated space, parking spaces, their parts in Republican property', 'Regulations on the Procedure for Determining the Amount of Rent in Renting Capital Structures (Buildings), Isolated Space, Parking Spaces, Their Parts', 'Regulations on the Procedure for Determining the Amount of Rent in Renting Capital Structures (Buildings, Structures), Isolated Premises, their Parts in Markets and Shopping Centres for the Organization and Implementation of the Retail Trade', 'Regulations on the Procedure for Determining the Amount of Rent in Renting Equipment, Vehicles Owned by the State') // The National Register of Legal Acts of Belarus, 4 Apr. 2012, No. 39, 1/13414.
45. *See, e.g.*, Regulation of the Ministry of Sports and Tourism of the Republic of Belarus of 22 Jul. 2013, No. 19 'On Approval of the Model Provisions on Urban, Regional Fitness Centre (the Centre of Sports and Recreation Activities), Sports Clubs' // The National Legal Internet Portal of the Republic of Belarus, 23 Aug. 2013, 8/27810.
46. Regulation of the Council of Ministers on 21 Jul. 2006, No. 916 'On Measures for Further Improvement of Mass Physical Culture and Sports Activities' // The National Register of Legal Acts of Belarus, 2 Aug. 2006, No. 122, 5/22627.

Subject activities (including enterprises), according to constituent documents, are:

(1) Development of physical training and (or) sports.
(2) Preparation of sports reserves and (or) sportspeople of a high class.
(3) Sport-improving and (or) mass sport work.
(4) Carrying out sports actions and (or) participating in them, including preparing and representing sportspeople on its own behalf at sports competitions.
(5) Methodical maintenance of systems of physical training and sport.
(6) Prevention of doping in sport and organization of doping controls (Article 16 of LPCS).

145. The requirements to become the director of a sports club of a higher educational institution are high enough. The director organizes and coordinates work for all activities of the sports club, provides and is responsible for the development of sport-improving and mass sport work in an educational institution, controls the organization and safety of pupils engaging in training processes in sports sections, groups and national teams, researches and introduces new forms and methods of sport-improving work and manages the financial and economic activity of the sports club. The director of the sports club should know relevant legal acts, supervise methodical documents and materials concerning the formation, direction and prospects for the development of physical training and sports and understand the features of the structure of a sports club, the basics of pedagogics, psychology and physiology, the theories and techniques for organizing sport-improving work, economy and the work and management of an organization, the basics of organizing financial and economic activities, the basics of labour legislation and the rules and norms of labour and fire safety.[47]

§8. Competition Rules

146. Sports competitions in Belarus, except for official championships, can be held by state bodies, organizations and citizens (persons holding competitions). Sports competitions can be official and unofficial (Article 42(1) LPCS).

147. The official sports competitions of Belarus are held according to republican and local planned schedules for carrying out official sports competitions. The republican planned schedule for carrying out official sports competitions is approved by the Ministry of Sports and Tourism of Belarus. Local planned schedules for carrying out official sports competitions are approved by local executive and administrative bodies (Article 42(2)(3) LPCS). Sports competitions are held according to provisions on carrying out competitions by the type/s of sport and the confirmed persons holding the competitions (Article 43(1) LPCS).

---

47. About some measures on preparation of the Belarus sportsmen for Olympic and Paralympic Games 2004 and 2006: the Decree of President of Republic of Belarus, 22 Jan. 2004 // The National Register of Legal Acts of Belarus, 2 Feb. 2004, No. 18, 1/5270.

148. All rights to broadcasting sports competitions belong to the competition organizers unless otherwise provided for in the instructions of the President of the Republic of Belarus, in a contract between the competition organizers and sports-related organizations representing a sportsperson (or team) (if there is no relevant sports-related organization) or in competition rules (Article 45(1) LPCS).

149. Within a calendar year, one official championship of Belarus per type of sport and one official competition for a cup among sportspeople of each level, except for the type/s of sports specified in point 5 of the present article, as a rule, can be played (Article 44(4) LPCS).

150. In sport types where competitions take place indoors and in open air, within a calendar year, the official championships of Belarus can take place in winter and in summer (Article 44(5) LPCS).

151. The official championships and cups of Belarus can be organized by national federations (unions, associations), as well as the Ministry of Sports and Tourism and other state bodies according to their competence, or the organizations authorized by them (Article 21(7) LPCS).

152. Organizations and citizens have the right to take part in international sports competitions taking place in the territory of Belarus and its limits, with observance of the requirements established by the persons holding the competition and not contradicting the legislation of Belarus (Article 72(4) LPCS).

153. The Ministry of Sports and Tourism of Belarus, other state bodies, as well as the organizations authorized by them, including the NOC of Belarus, the PC of Belarus and national federations (unions, associations) by type of sport have the right and the competence to represent the interests of Belarus in international sports organizations, as well as in the sporting and other actions taken by international sports organizations (Article 73(1) LPCS).

154. The persons holding the competitions define refereeing for sports competitions, including international competitions (Article 46(1) LPCS).

155. Refereeing of Belarusian official sports competitions is carried out only by judges of sport (Article 46(2) LPCS).

156. The procedure and payment for refereeing of sports competitions are at the expense of the republican and (or) local budgets set by the Ministry of Sports and Tourism in coordination with the Ministry of Finance of the Republic of Belarus and the regional (Minsk) executive committees (Article 46(3) LPCS).

§9. Supporters' Rights

I. The Right of Sports Supporters to Safety During Sports Actions

157. The right of sports fans to safety during sports actions is basic in the general system of the rights of sports supporters. The right to safety (including for sports fans) in Belarus is fixed at a legislative level in Article 5 of the LPCS.

158. The Resolution of the Ministry of Sports and Tourism of 31 August 2018, No. 60, confirms the safety rules for conducting physical training and sports actions (hereinafter 'the Rules'),[48] which establishes the requirements for security measures when conducting physical training and sports actions, including sports competitions and training gatherings. It also defines the duties of citizens and organizations in the maintenance of safe conduct of physical training and sport. These rules are obligatory for all territories of Belarus and extend to citizens and organizations, irrespective of the organizational-legal form and pattern of ownership. Conditions at which present sports competitions are held, in particular:

(1) Sports constructions should be operated in the order established by the legislation.
(2) The presence of documents regulating the order of their operation and rules for conducting sports competitions by type of sport is confirmed when due hereunder by the organization (citizen) holding these sporting competitions.
(3) Weather conditions do not represent a health hazard to sportspeople engaged in physical training, as well as the spectators (sports fans).
(4) Sports constructions should conform to sanitary and hygiene norms.

159. In separate standard legal acts, the right of sports fans to safety during sports actions is realized by the establishment of the duty to observe certain safety rules and also by the establishment of certain restrictions and interdictions. In the Law of Belarus of 30 December 1997, No. 114-Z (updated version: 24 May 2021) 'On Mass Actions in Belarus' (Law No. 114-Z),[49] the duty of participants in mass actions (including sport) is established to maintain public order and meet all legal requirements for the organizers of the mass action, employees of law-enforcement bodies and the representatives of the public who carry out duties to protect public order.

160. Law No. 114-Z contains the norms forbidding participants and organizers of mass action to take certain actions. For example, during mass actions, it is forbidden for organizers and participants: to interfere with the movement of transport and pedestrians, to have on their person knifes, fire, gas, weapons, explosives, ammunition, items whose destructive effect is based on the use of combustible substances, their imitations and fakes, other items that can be used as weapons, poisonous, corrosive, noxious or flammable substances, flammable and pyrotechnic

48. The National Register of Legal Acts of Belarus, 25 Sep. 2018, No. 8/33467.
49. The National Register of Legal Acts of Belarus, 21 Aug. 2003, No. 93, 2/982.

substances or products (except matches and pocket lighters), other substances, objects and products, including homemade, that may produce smoke or fire, as well as alcoholic and low-alcohol beverages and (or) beer or to act in ways that threaten public safety, or the life and health of participants of the specified action or other persons.

161. Law No. 114 Z establishes that the sale of alcoholic beverages and beer during mass events is carried out taking into account the prohibitions and restrictions established by law. In particular, the Law of the Republic of Belarus of 27.08.2008 N 429-3 (updated version: 15.07.2021) 'On State Regulation of the Production and Turnover of Alcoholic, Non-food Alcohol-containing Products and Non-food Ethyl Alcohol' establishes restrictions connected with alcoholic drinks and beer. For example, consumption of alcoholic drinks and beer in places conducting mass actions, and in a radius of territories adjoining them of 500 metres, is forbidden for two hours prior to the beginning and for the period of these actions for the organizations and persons who are not organizers and participants, except for the consumption of alcoholic drinks and beer within specific organizations.

II. The Right of Sports Supporters to Acquire Tickets to Sport Actions

162. One of the problems for state bodies, the subjects of enterprise activity rendering services in the field of physical training and sport and other interested bodies, is improving the mechanism of ticket sales for sports actions and improving state control over the realization of this.

163. For the first time, questions on ticket distribution were considered at the state level after the exit of the football club BATE in a group round of the UEFA Champions League. In particular, for the BATE versus Juventus match on 15 October 2008, entrance tickets were on sale on 16 September 2008. Their cost ranged from 5,000 to 30,000 Belarusian roubles (BYN). Tickets were distributed as follows: about 30% were realized through the Dynamo stadium cash desks, about 30% went on sale at the Barysaŭ city stadium, about 35% were allocated for realization by the organizations under the clearing settlement and about 5% were allocated for realization by Italian fans. There were no tickets left for realization at the cash desks of Barysaŭ and Minsk on 17 September 2008. However, there were no restrictions on their realization. Tickets were bought by speculators in unlimited quantities and realized at several times more than their face value. Sports fans could not realize their right to attend sporting action. The disorganization taking place in the realization of tickets for the BATE matches against Zenith and Juventus led to disorders at the Dynamo stadium and the Dynamo cash desks in Minsk.

164. Despite the fact that the Ministry of Sports and Tourism had developed a standard legal certificate regulating the manufacturing and distribution of entrance tickets for sports competitions in Belarus, problems of ticket realization for sporting actions have not been resolved.

III. The Right of Sports Supporters to Compensation for Harm Caused During the Organization and Conduct of Sports Actions

165. In Belarus, the Decree of the President of Belarus from 25 August 2006, No. 530, 'On Insurance Activity' (updated version: 11 May 2019, No. 175)[50] defines the types of obligatory insurance. These include obligatory insurance of civil liability for owners of vehicles, obligatory insurance of civil liability of a passenger carrier and obligatory insurance for manufacturing accidents and occupational diseases. The major problem for state bodies (the Ministry of Sports and Tourism of Belarus and the Ministry of Finance of Belarus) is the need for obligatory insurance, which is the responsibility of the organizers of mass sporting actions. The object of insurance, insurance claims, the size of insurance payments, the insurance sums (responsibility limits), insurance risks and the system of financing should be in the regulated details.

IV. Other Rights of Sports Supporters

166. Sports supporters can be divided into two categories: active and passive. Active sports fans are the physical persons directly visiting the sporting event. Passive sports fans are the physical persons satisfying their interest by means of viewing sports actions through mass media (TV, internet, etc.).

167. The right of passive sports fans to the viewing of sporting actions in Belarus is realized by means of the Law of Belarus of 10 May 2007, No. 225-Z (updated version: 4 January 2021) 'On Advertising'.[51] In particular, Article 11(4) of the given law has provided that translation occurs on air or in the recording of a sports competition and the competition can only be interrupted by advertising in breaks or during stops. Transmission, either live or in recorded form, of sports competitions in which breaks or stops are not provided can be interrupted by advertising so that translation interruption does not lead to loss of essential information for the sports competition.

168. The basic discontent of sports supporters is reduced to the following:

(1) The bad organization of the sporting action.
(2) The disrespectful actions of persons engaged in protecting public order during a sporting action.
(3) Insufficiently developed networks of points of sale for fast food and sports souvenirs.

50. The National Register of Legal Acts of Belarus, 6 Sep. 2006, No. 143, 1/7866.
51. The National Register of Legal Acts of Belarus, 21 May 2007, No. 119, 2/1321.

§10. SPORTS FOR HANDICAPPED INDIVIDUALS

169. Belarus operates the largest world sporting movement for handicapped and adaptive sport, including the Paralympics (for persons with infringement of sight and the musculoskeletal system), the Deaflympics and the Special Olympics. According to the given directions, the national adaptive sporting organizations exercising public administration include:

(1) The PC, which was created in 1996 and was recognized by the International Paralympic Committee in 1997; the Federation of Physical Training and Sport of the Belarusian Association of the Sight Handicapped for sporting activities for those handicapped in their sight; the Belarusian Federation of Physical Training and Sport for Handicapped Individuals for sport among handicapped individuals with infringements of the musculoskeletal system.
(2) The Belarusian Sports Federation of Deaf Persons (BSFDP) was created in 1992 and since 1993 has been a member of the International Committee of Sports for the Deaf (CISS), the International Committee of Silent Chess (ICSC) and the European Deaf Sport Organization (EDSO).
(3) The Belarusian Special Olympics Committee (BSOC) operates the national programme for Special Olympics, and it was recognized by the international Olympic movement in 1992.

170. Article 7 of the LPCS contains the concept of the term 'the Paralympic movement of Belarus', which is defined as a part of the international Paralympic movement. The purposes of this are the promotion of the development of physical culture and sports for people with disorders of the musculoskeletal system and infringements of sight, strengthening the international sporting cooperation of handicapped sportspeople and representing the Republic of Belarus at the Paralympic Games and other international sporting events held with the participation of these people. The directions for handicapped sportspeople are stated in Article 52 of the LPCS.

171. In Chapter 5 of the LPCS, 'General Provisions on Sport', directions for adaptive sports are not mentioned. The LPCS, as a subject of legal regulation, does not consider the sport of disabled people and mass sport work with disabled people, noting only that it is directed to increase their impellent activity and is a component of the rehabilitation of disabled individuals. Article 34 of Chapter 4 'Physical Training' defines the system of state bodies that organize the sport-improving and mass sport work with disabled individuals, including children with delayed psychophysical development, and engage in sport-improving and mass sport work with disabled individuals, together with the PC, physical training and sports organizations and other organizations conducting activities in this sphere. This system includes the Ministry of Education of Belarus, the Ministry of Health of Belarus, the Ministry of Sports and Tourism, the Ministry of Labour and Social Protection of Belarus, local executive and administrative bodies and other state bodies according to their competence.

172. The concept of a 'disability' and the recognition of a person with a disability is defined in the Law of Belarus dated 11 November 1991, No. 1224-XII, 'About Social Protection of the Disabled People in Belarus' (updated version: 16 November 2010).[52] A person with a disability is defined as a person with a steady physical, mental, intellectual or sensory infringement that causes various barriers to full and effective participation in society on a level with other citizens. The recognition of a disability is conducted by a doctorial-rehabilitation commission of experts.

§11. Public Safety

173. In the legislation of Belarus, the term safety, in relation to the physical training and sporting sphere, is used in Article 5 of the LPCS 'Physical Training and Sport Safety Rules'. The Council of Ministers of Belarus issued a Resolution dated 5 May 2014, No. 426 (updated version: 25 May 2018, No. 394) 'About Delegation to the Ministry of Sports and Tourism of Powers on Acceptance of Legal Acts',[53] which authorizes the Ministry of Sports and Tourism to issue statements regarding safety rules for conducting physical training and sport. These safety rules are confirmed by the decision of the Ministry of Sports and Tourism of Belarus dated 31 August 2018, No. 60.[54] These rules establish requirements for security measures when engaged in physical training and sport employment, including sports competitions and training gatherings. It also defines the duties of citizens and organizations for the maintenance of safe conduct of such employment, creating conditions for health protection, prevention of trauma, completing organizational-preventive measures for maintaining safety within sports constructions and in times and places of conducting physical training and sport employment. The rules mention separate aspects of considered problems and anything else required to meet the full requirements of the regulation.

174. The safety of a person engaging in physical training and sport is the condition of securing the life and health of that person from internal and external threats, which can arise in connection with challenges created by society for the realization of impellent activity with a focus on strengthening health and engaging in competitive activities and activities in preparation for competitions (training process), as well as the system of the measures for the timely discovery and elimination of internal and external threats.

175. The subjects responsible for safety in physical training and sport are the state in the name of its legislative, executive and judicial bodies, physical training and sports organizations, physical training collectives and sportspeople and visitors to sporting events (spectators, fans).

52. The National Register of Legal Acts of Belarus, 24 Jul. 2009, No. 173, 2/1600.
53. The National Register of Legal Acts of Belarus, 7 May 2014, No. 5/38812.
54. The National Register of Legal Acts of Belarus, 25 Sep. 2018, No. 8/33467.

176. The order of conducting mass actions is regulated by the Law of Belarus dated 30 December 1997 (updated version: 24 May 2021) 'On Mass Actions in the Republic of Belarus'.[55] The mass sports action are only '… spent in the places specially not intended for this purpose open-air or indoors' (Article 2). While conducting such actions (Article 11), it is forbidden for organizers and participants to:

(1) interfere with the movement of vehicles and pedestrians;
(2) hinder the uninterrupted functioning of the organization;
(3) establish tents or other shoddy constructions;
(4) influence, in any form, employees of law-enforcement bodies with a view of hindering their performance of official duties and representatives of the public who are carrying out duties to protect the public order;
(5) have on their person weapons, explosives, ammunition and their simulations and models; other items that can be used as weapons; poisonous, pungently smelling or fire-accelerant substances; flammable and pyrotechnic substances or products other than matches and pocket lighters; other substances, objects and products, including self-made items, the use of which can lead to smoke contamination or ignition; as well as alcohol, low-alcohol drinks and (or) beer;
(6) carry out propaganda of war or extremist activity, including the use of posters, headers or other means;
(7) create threats to public safety or to the life and health of participants or other persons, or to hide their person under masks;
(8) use flags and pendants not registered in accordance with established procedures and to use emblems, symbols, posters and banners aimed at causing damage to public order, rights and the legitimate interests of citizens;
(9) make any actions breaking the established order of the organization and the mass activity and to incite such actions by any methods.

§12. Tobacco Ban

177. According to Article 31 of the Decree of the President of the Republic of Belarus, No. 28, dated 17 December 2002 (updated version: 16 November 2020) 'On the State Regulation of Production, Turnover and Consumption of Tobacco Material and Tobacco Goods',[56] the retail trade of tobacco products is forbidden in sports constructions and in their territories, as well as in the buildings of sports organizations.

178. According to Article 35 of the Decree of the President of the Republic of Belarus, No. 28, smoking is prohibited in sports institutions, with the exception of special places.

55. The National Register of Legal Acts of Belarus, 21 Aug. 2003, No. 93, 2/982.
56. The National Register of Legal Acts of Belarus, 26 Dec. 2002, No. 143, 1/4234.

§13. Criminal Law

179. Article 253 of the Criminal Code of Belarus dated 9 July 1999, No. 275-Z (updated version: 26 May 2021)[57] 'Payoff of Participants and Organizers of Sports Competitions or Commercial Entertainment Competitions' states that the reception of money, securities, property or services by the sportsperson, the coach, the medical worker participating in the sports training of a sportsperson (a team of sportspeople), the sports judge, the sports agent, another person included in the participants of a sporting competition, the organizer of a sporting competition or the organizer or judge of a commercial entertainment competition for rendering an influence on the results of a competition, for committing a predetermined action (inaction) during a sporting competition or a commercial entertainment competition, or the granting of such compensation are punished by penalty or by deprivation of the right to occupy certain positions or be engaged in certain activities or correctional labour for the term of up to two years, or arrest or restriction of freedom for a term of up to three years, or imprisonment for the same term.

180. The same actions made repeatedly are punished by penalty or restriction of freedom for a term of up to four years, or with imprisonment for the same term, either with or without a deprivation of the right to occupy certain positions or be engaged in certain activities. According to the official note to the article, in certain cases, the person who provided the remuneration is exempt from criminal liability. In particular, if the remuneration was paid by a person due to extortion or if this person voluntarily reported what he had done and actively contributed to the disclosure or investigation of the crime.

§14. Financing

181. Article 65 of the LPCS 'Physical Training and Sports Financing' establishes that the financing of physical training and sport is carried out at the expense of the republican and local budgets, the physical training and sports organizations and other sources not forbidden by legislation.

182. The Decree of the President dated 15 April 2013, No. 190 (updated version: 9 September 2019, No. 329) 'On Measures to Encourage Achievement of High Sports Results' (together with the 'Regulations on the Procedure for Appointment and Payment of Scholarships of the President of the Republic of Belarus in the Field of Physical Training and Sport' and the 'Regulations on the Procedure of Distribution of Prizes in Cash or In-kind Payment to Athletes and Coaches')[58] regulates the financing of the most outstanding athletes and the order of prizes for athletes and rewards for coaches.

---

57. The National Register of Legal Acts of Belarus, 15 Oct. 1999, No. 76, 2/50.
58. The National Legal Internet Portal of the Republic of Belarus, 18 Apr. 2013, 1/14217.

183. According to Decree No. 190, scholarships can be assigned and paid to athletes and coaches who are:

(1) on the national team of the Republic of Belarus for a particular sport (national teams);
(2) the athlete instructor;
(3) the head coach, senior coach, coach, team head, trainer, administrator, instructor, doctor, trainer, massage therapist, psychologist, veterinarian, engineer or trainer-mechanic.

184. Prizes in cash or in-kind payment are awarded to athletes and the coaches who participated in their preparation for the following sports achievements:

(1) Winning medals at the Olympics, Paralympics and Deaflympics, World and European Championships, World Cups for team sports or World University Games.
(2) Setting world, European or Belarusian records for adult athletes in Olympic, Paralympic, Deaflympic and non-Olympic sports.
(3) Winning or earning a draw in a final match of the Olympic Games, World and European Championships and World Cups in team sports.

185. The size of prizes for athletes who won medals at the Olympics, Paralympics and Deaflympics, and rewards for coaches who provided athletes with training, is established by the President of the Republic of Belarus.

186. Prizes are given only for the first place in international sports competitions, such as badminton, boxing, freestyle wrestling, Greco-Roman wrestling, judo, karate, kickboxing, sambo, archery, taekwondo, Thai boxing, tennis, table tennis, martial arts and fencing, which involve seven athletes from seven countries, and in international sporting events for other sports, which include five athletes (teams) from five countries. The prizes are not provided when competing with fewer athletes and (or) teams from other countries.

187. In team sports (team games, team and group exercises, relays, etc.), every athlete is awarded in the manner and under the conditions specified for the individual sports in international sports competitions. The prizes are not given for team results when athletes and teams are not awarded medals.

188. Coaches who participate in the preparation of athletes and national teams of the Republic of Belarus for sports (except sports with no full-time national teams) include:

(1) Coaches of the national sporting teams of the Republic of Belarus (national teams) working under a contract with the Ministry of Sports and Tourism or exercising duties as a coach from among servicemen, officers and other ranks of the Investigative Committee, of the Interior Office, of the State Control

Committee (the Department of Financial Investigations) and agencies and departments for emergency situations registered in national teams, including state coaches of national teams.

(2) Personal coaches of athletes working directly with the athletes for at least one year at the time of participation in international sporting events, as well as trainers for related types of training (in sports from the first group in accordance with the law).

(3) Coaches providing athletes with training at an early stage, teachers in specialized educational and sports institutions, secondary schools and schools for Olympic reserves and coaches in other physical culture and sports organizations who have worked with the athlete/s for at least two years.

189. In non-Olympic sports, as well as the Paralympic and Deaflympic disciplines, the rewards for coaches mentioned above are paid only for the preparation of athletes who have signed contracts with the Ministry of Sports and Tourism or when exercising duties as a coach from among servicemen, officers and other ranks of the Investigative Committee, of the Interior Office, of the State Control Committee (the Department of Financial Investigations) and agencies and departments for emergency situations that are registered in the national teams, including the state coaches of national teams.

190. The Decree of the President of the Republic of Belarus dated 15 April 2013, No. 191 (updated version: 29 December 2020, No. 497) 'On Support to Organizations of Physical Culture and Sport'[59] is important for the financing of sports in Belarus.

191. According to Decree No. 191, support for the organization of physical culture and sport under the list in Appendix 1[60] (sports organizations) is in the form of donation by legal entities and individual entrepreneurs to the sports organizations, in accordance with the law and with the specifications established by the Decree. This includes funds (payment for goods, works or services) for sports organizations under contract on the transfer of the debt, gratuitous services (works) and (or) the gratuitous transfer of property, including property rights, with the inclusion of the cost of providing such gratuitous assistance tax purposes. Typically, the donation does not cover clubs of any type/s of sport and other organizations of physical culture and sport, teams that do not participate in the top leagues (in ice hockey – in the extra league) of championships of the Republic of Belarus and (or) championships of other states.

59. The national legal Internet portal of the Republic of Belarus, 17 Apr. 2013, 1/14218.

60. The list of sports organizations that receive state support is: National Olympic Committee of Belarus Public Association 'The Paralympic Committee of the Republic of Belarus', Republican Federation (unions, associations) in sports included in the Olympic programme, the Belarusian Collegiate Athletic Association, Chamber of Commerce and Private Unitary Enterprise 'Belarusian Biathlon Club' Clubs.

192. Support under Decree No. 191 can be in the form of subsidies from the local budgets in consideration of the requirements set out in paragraph 4 of the Decree. However, this rule does not cover club levels of sports and other organizations of physical culture and sports and teams that participate in championships of the Republic of Belarus and (or) championships of other states for baseball, futsal and motoball.

193. State support under Decree No. 191 may take the form of rights to sports organizations, created in the form of public associations (unions) to carry out, in accordance with paragraph 11 of Decree No. 191, types of entrepreneurial activity[61] without the formation of business entities and (or) participation in them.

194. In accordance with Decree No. 191, state support may be in the form of tax incentives, in the form of providing legal entities and individual entrepreneurs with gratuitous (sponsor) assistance in accordance with the Decree of the President of Belarus dated 1 July 2005, No. 300 (updated version: 10 May 2019, No. 169) 'On the Provision and Use of Gratuitous (Sponsor) Assistance',[62] and in other forms, in accordance with the law:

(1) Mandatory conditions giving sports clubs and other organizations of physical culture and sport and teams that participate in championships of Belarus and (or) championships of other states for basketball, baseball, volleyball, water polo, handball, mini-football, motoball, beach volleyball, field hockey, ice hockey, football (hereinafter 'sports clubs') the right to receive support in accordance with Decree No. 191 as sponsorship from government organizations, provided the existing agreed plans for the development of sports clubs are approved by the local executive and administrative authorities in which these clubs operate.

(2) Quarterly providing (no later than the 20th day of the month following the reporting quarter) reports on the costs of sports clubs to the local executive and administrative bodies where these clubs are situated; Since 2017, support for sports clubs has been in accordance with paragraphs 1.1–1.4 of Decree No. 191, as well as sub-paragraph 1.5 of Decree No. 191, which states that the grant sponsorship from government agencies is given in an amount not exceeding the income from entrepreneurial activity, international sports organizations and transfer deals that the club received in the previous year, with the exception of sports clubs that have achieved high results in European club competitions in the Continental Hockey League and Youth Hockey league for 2017.

61. Sports organizations, created in the form of public associations (unions, associations), are entitled to exercise without formation of business entities and (or) their participation in the following types of business: (1) sports activities; (2) tourist activity; (3) wholesale and retail trade; (4) promotional activities; (5) other activities, recreation and entertainment; (6) hire other household and personal items; (7) water transport activities; (8) activities of other land passenger transport, non-scheduled; (9) services of car parks; (10) construction; (11) publishing; (12) printing and service activities in this area; (13) web portal activities

62. The National Register of Legal Acts of Belarus, 2005, No. 105, 1/6586.

(3) At least 25% of funds, goods, services and assets, including property rights, obtained by sports clubs in accordance with Decree No. 191 as a grant (sponsor) from government organizations, should be used for directing the development of youth sports and the infrastructure of the sport, including at least 15% directed towards the development of youth sports.

195. Under Decree No. 191, gratuitous assistance (sponsorship) may be provided to sports organizations step-by-step, in accordance with the schedule set in the grant contract concluded between the sports organizations as legal entities and individual entrepreneurs providing such support.

196. Local executive and administrative authorities, where these sports clubs are situated, have the right to use local budgets to support clubs in the form of grants for partial funding (no more than 40% of the amount of funds calculated on the basis of norms and standards for budgetary organizations), in accordance with the list of types of costs for supporting sports clubs set out in Annex 2 to Decree No. 191.[63] At the same time, allocations from local budget funds can be tended to sports clubs for one or more types of expenses listed in Annex 2 to Decree No. 191.

197. Costs for the formation of sports clubs are determined on the basis of schedules for sporting events, consistent with the regional and district (city) departments of physical culture and sport for the local executive and administrative authorities. Costs are approved by the heads of these clubs in consultation with the local executive and administrative authorities.

198. According to Article 5 of Decree No. 191, the money, works, services and property, including property rights, obtained by sports organizations in accordance with Decree No. 191, as well as funds released from tax benefits provided by Decree No. 191, are used by:

(1) The NOC of the Republic of Belarus, the PC of the Republic of Belarus, the Belarusian Association of University Sports and the public association Belarusian Sports Federation of the Deaf for the realization of their goals (objectives).
(2) The national sports federations (unions, associations) included in the Olympic programme and the trade-production unitary enterprise, the Belarusian Biathlon Club, in accordance with the budgets agreed by the Ministry of Sports and Tourism for the development of the respective sports and the list of cost types for supporting national federations (unions, associations) involved with sports included in the Olympic programme and the Belarusian Biathlon Club, according to Annex 3.
(3) Sports clubs, according to the estimates agreed to by local executive and administrative bodies, with regard to the conditions set out in paragraph 2 of

63. 'List of Types of Costs for Supporting Clubs in Team Sports' is not given here.

this Decree on the implementation of its statutory goals (tasks) and in accordance with Annex 2 of this Decree on the development of youth and sports infrastructure.

199. Sports clubs use these funds in the realization of their statutory objectives (tasks), in accordance with Annex 2 to Decree No. 191, as agreed by the local executive and administrative authorities, where these clubs are situated. The support and funds from other sources cannot be used by sports organizations for purposes defined as income derived from business activity.

200. Plans for the development of sports clubs are approved annually by the local executive and administrative authorities where these clubs are situated, as well as coordinated with the relevant national sports federations (unions, associations) and the Ministry of Sports and Tourism. These plans should include:

(1) Income from all sources, including the income derived from business activities and their costs.
(2) Development of the structure of the club, including the main team and youth team, youth sports schools (specialized youth schools for Olympic reserves) and sports facilities.
(3) The development of youth sports, including training of reserve players in youth sports schools (specialized youth schools for Olympic reserves), in a separate structural unit of sports clubs and other sports schools dependent on contractual conditions.
(4) Information on the existing (planned) financial contractual obligations to each athlete and coach of the club's team in game sports participating in the higher league (in ice hockey – in the extra league) of the championship of the Republic of Belarus and (or) championships, cup draws of other states, as well as the amounts of money paid to sports agents in the previous year (planned to be paid this year).

201. Sports organizations have the right to:

(1) Dispose of funds received from legal entities and individual entrepreneurs in Belarusian banks.
(2) Transfer assets, including transfers of gratuitous funds and the rights to television, radio and other means of sports broadcasting and sell tickets to sporting events held by them or with their participation.
(3) Rent and own real estate.

202. Sports organizations, created in the form of voluntary associations (unions, associations), are entitled to carry out the following types of business activity without the creation of commercial organizations or participation in such organizations:

(1) Sports activities
(2) Tourist activities

(3) Wholesale and retail trade
(4) Promotional activities
(5) Other recreational and entertainment activities
(6) Rent household goods and personal items
(7) Transport via water
(8) Non-scheduled land-based passenger transport
(9) Car park services
(10) Construction
(11) Publishing
(12) Printing and related services in this area.
(13) Web portal activity

203. Legal entities and individual entrepreneurs supporting sports organizations have the right to:

(1) provide unlimited assistance to sports organizations on the basis of the contract of gratuitous (sponsor) assistance;
(2) not specify in contracts the types of goods (works, services) that will be purchased by sports organizations (made, rendered for them) at the expense of these funds in the process of providing a grant aid (sponsorship) in the form of cash.

204. The gross profit of sports organizations is reduced by the amount of profit used for the purposes set out in paragraph 5 of Decree No. 191 (statutory sports purposes).

205. Sports organizations are exempt from the following taxes:

(1) Tax on the profits received by sports organizations from advertising.
(2) Income tax for individuals on surcharges on food for athlete-instructors and trainees in excess of the standards during training camps and sports events, up to 25% of their annual salary at their main place of work.
(3) Value-added tax on imports into the territory of the Republic of Belarus (with the exception of sports clubs that do not participate in European club competitions, competitions held by international sports federations, the Continental Hockey League and the Youth Hockey league); imports include general and special purpose sportswear and footwear, sports equipment, tools, other equipment (including small boats, boats, outboard motors, dinghies and parts), sporting guns and ammunition, sports horses and vehicles for the transport of horses intended for their own needs. This includes the national teams of Belarus, specialized educational and sports institutions, secondary schools (including schools for Olympic reserves in their respective sports), as well as for the territory of Belarus when hosting international sports events (championships, World Cups and European Cups). This rule applies to clubs participating in European club tournaments in game sports (organized by international sports federations, the Continental Hockey League and the Youth

Hockey League) from the moment they become eligible to participate in such events and during the year following the sporting season in which the club participated in these sporting events.

§15. Tax

206. General provisions of the tax laws of Belarus are contained in the Tax Code of Belarus (Special Part) dated 29 December 2009, No. 71-Z (updated version: 29 December 2020).[64]

I. Value-Added Tax (VAT)

207. Article 118 (1.6) of the Tax Code (TC) exempts the turnover of goods (works, services) and property rights of specialized sports establishments used for the training of student athletes from value-added tax.

II. Profit Tax

208. In accordance with Article 174 of the TC 'Extraordinary Charges', which reduces the taxable base, the structure of non-operating expenses includes organization expenses in the form of a difference between the sum of expenses for the maintenance of educational establishments being on their balance, houses for elderly and disabled individuals, objects of available housing, public health services, culture establishments and sport, and the sum of incomes connected with the operation of specified establishments and objects received by the organizations. Thus, expenses are considered in an order established by the present chapter. The present position is applied for expenses at the individual share level of the organization in the maintenance of specified establishments and objects and not applied for their exclusive use in enterprise activity.

209. According to Article 173 (1.3) of the TC, expenses are not considered for employment payments at clubs and cultural-entertainment and sporting events.

210. Article 181 (1) of the TC establishes the profits exempt from the tax on profits. The TC excludes from tax the profits of organizations (at a rate of no more than 10% of total profit determined for the tax period in which the profit is transferred), registered in the territory of Belarus, including public health services, social security, culture, physical culture and sport, religious organizations and public associations (including the Belarusian Society of Disabled People, the Belarusian Society of Deaf Persons and the Belarusian Association of the Visually Handicapped),

64. The National Register of Legal Acts of Belarus, 31 Dec. 2018, No. 2/2594.

their unitary enterprises, or used on the payment of invoices for goods received and transferred to the specified organizations (works, services) and the release of property rights.

III. Personal Income Tax

211. According to Article 196(2) of the TC, objects of taxation from physical persons are not admitted as incomes, received by payers:

(1) At a rate of payment set by the organizations, including trade union organizations or individual businesspeople, for expenses accrued when conducting mass sports actions.
(2) At a rate dependent on the type of sport.

212. The following incomes are released from surtax from physical persons:

(1) all incomes identified by the acts and decisions of the Council of Ministers of Belarus;
(2) payments for the cost of food, sports equipment and sport and dress uniforms received by sportspeople and employees of the sporting organizations for training processes and participation in sports competitions (Article 196(2.4) TC);
(3) prizes received by sportspeople for participating in international and domestic competitions, monetary rewards for coaches and other specialists who took part in the training of these sportspeople, as well as prizes received by winners of domestic competitions, as defined by the President of Belarus and (or) the Council of Ministers of the Republic of Belarus (Article 208(25) TC).

213. The size of the tax base is defined in Article 199(3) of the TC. The following categories of taxpayers have the right to apply professional tax deductions:

> Taxpayers and their coaches receiving personal activity incomes for participation in commercial sporting competitions (games, performances), provided that such activity is carried out by taxpayers, not within the limits of team participation; this includes such incomes and documentarily confirmed expenses directly connected with the realization of the following activities:
>
> (1) Payments for the journey to a place of competition and back;
> (2) Payments for residing at the place of participation in competitions;
> (3) Payments for sports equipment and sport and full dress uniforms. (Article 212(2) TC).

214. The decision of the Council of Ministers of Belarus dated 28 January 2009, No. 111 'On the Statement of the List of Types of Activities of Educational Institutions and Establishments Providing Vocational Training, in Which the Incomes

Received by Pupils Are Released from Surtax on Physical Persons'[65] (updated version: 15 February 2013) establishes that pupils receiving an income for sports activities are released from surtax on physical persons.

IV. Real Estate Tax

215. During service delivery by organizations and individual businesspeople, rent and other gratuitous use of buildings and constructions (their parts) are released from real estate tax; the buildings and constructions (their parts) of budgetary organizations are subject to real estate tax, according to Article 228(2) of the TC.

216. The following buildings and constructions (their parts), leased car parking places are not subject to real estate tax:

(1) establishments financed from the budget of organizations and individual businesspeople responsible for training children and teenagers in specialized sports establishments;
(2) specialized sports schools of trade unions financed at the expense of state social insurance.

V. Land Tax

217. The following are released from land tax under Article 239 of the TC:

(1) The ground areas of organizations carrying out welfare activities and receiving grants from government budgets, trade union organizations of Belarus carrying out welfare activities and sanatoriums and organizations engaged in youth sports-improving work and sporting schools, irrespective of ownership, when the grounds are used for the realization of authorized activity.
(2) The ground areas of organizations occupied with sports constructions, being bases for preparing the national and international sporting teams of Belarus.
(3) The ground areas of public associations for disabled individuals (their private unitary enterprises and establishments), occupied with objects of physical training and sport.

218. Calculation and payment of ground tax are not required under tenancy or other gratuitous use of buildings, constructions (their parts) or car parking places for:

(1) Budgetary organizations.
(2) Organizations engaged in social and cultural activities that receive subsidies from the budget.

65. The National Register of Legal Acts of Belarus, 6 Feb. 2009, No. 31, 5/29220.

(3) Specialized educational and sports institutions of trade unions funded by state social insurance.
(4) Organizations providing sports facilities that are the main basis for preparing the national teams of the Republic of Belarus by type of sport.
(5) Educational institutions of consumer cooperatives – organizations and individual entrepreneurs responsible for pupil and student nutrition in educational institutions.

VI. Unified Tax

219. Unified tax is a kind of tax paid by individual entrepreneurs at a fixed rate depending on the type of commercial activity.

220. Individual businesspeople pay unified tax for physical comfort activities, which are activities in the field of sport (except for the activities involving the rental of recreational and sports equipment) (Article 337 TC):

Activity Type	*Base Rates of Uniform Tax for the Accounting Period BYN*				
	Minsk, the Minsk Area	*Brest and Hrodna*	*Vicebsk, Homiel and Mahiliou*	*Other Regional Cities*	*Other Settlements*
22. Physical comfort activities, including activities in the field of sport (with the exception of the rental of recreational and sports equipment)	50–60	60–85	75–85	40–70	35–50

§16. Dispute Settlement

221. Considering the fact that the legislation does not provide special jurisdictions for disputes resulting from sports relations, it is necessary to be guided by the general norms of the jurisdiction and the established remedial codes. Certainly, the jurisdiction of the general and economic courts will include considerations of disputes having civil, economic, labour or criminal characters.

222. When considering disputes of disciplinary character in sports federation disciplinary committees, these are guided by examples of disciplinary codes created by the relevant IF.

223. By adopting the law 'On Arbitration Courts'[66] in 2011, the Sport Arbitration Court was created by the public organization, the Union of Lawyers of Belarus.

66. The National Register of Legal Acts of Belarus, 25 Jul. 2011, No. 83, 2/1853.

Chapter 3. Private Regulations

224. The role of private regulations is taken away from the NOC and given to the national sports federations that operate in the frameworks defined by the international sports federations.

225. As a rule, national sports federations make legal acts of the following character:

(1) authorized federation documents;
(2) regulations for conducting competitions (championships) that are usually coordinated with the Ministry of Sports and Tourism;
(3) management requirements for licensing of clubs;
(4) codes of ethics;
(5) disciplinary codes;
(6) technical rules.

§1. NOC

226. The NOC of Belarus was created on 22 March 1991. On 9 March 1992, the NOC of Belarus was recognized by the IOC as a temporary member. At the 101st session of the IOC, which took place between 21 and 24 September 1993 in Monaco, the NOC of Belarus obtained official recognition. From that time, Belarus acquired the right to send national teams to the Olympic Games. The NOC of Belarus leads the Olympic movement of Belarus and participates in developing and implementing a uniform state policy for the development of higher achievements in sport, together with the Ministry of Sports and Tourism. In its activities, the NOC of Belarus is guided by the legislation of Belarus and the Olympic Charter of the IOC. The NOC recognizes:

(1) Thirty-six federations of summer Olympic sports
(2) Eight federations of winter Olympic sports.

227. There are also twenty-seven sports federations that are not included in the Olympic Games Programme but recognized by the NOC of Belarus, sixteen federations not included in the Olympic Games Programme and not recognized by the NOC of Belarus and two federations not included in the Olympic Games Programme but temporarily recognized by the NOC of Belarus.

228. The NOC of Belarus is represented in various regions. The structure of the NOC includes 104 members and 14 honorary members.

229. Under the decision of the NOC meeting of 26 January 1993, the NOC committee representatives in all the regional centres of Belarus and the city of Minsk should be engaged in distributing propaganda for the development of the Olympic movement; popularizing a healthy way of life and physical training for youth; developing mass sport; distributing propaganda against alcoholism, smoking and narcotics; providing sports equipment for children's homes; creating rehabilitation centres for sportspeople and opening schools for Olympic champions.

230. NOC representatives should promote state and social sports organizations and sports federations in the recruitment and preparation of sports reserves for national teams. The NOC is a public association and its status and role correspond to the Olympic Charter, the LPCS and the law 'On Public Associations'.

231. According to the Olympic Charter, the structure of the NOC includes:

(1) President.
(2) Vice-Presidents.
(3) Secretary General.
(4) NOC's Executive Committee.
(5) Revision Commission.
(6) NOC Representatives.
(7) Nine constant commissions that form the basis of the Olympic Committee:
   (i) the commission for the cooperation of the NOC's representatives;
   (ii) the commission on sportspeople's issues;
   (iii) the commission on culture, Olympic education and the development of university sports;
   (iv) the commission on 'Sport and Environment';
   (v) the commission on working with sports federations;
   (vi) the commission on legal issues;
   (vii) the commission on 'Women and Sport';
   (viii) the commission on working with mass media;
   (ix) the medical and anti-doping board.

232. The commissions are headed by members of the NOC Executive Committee.

233. The general structure of the NOC also includes members of Olympic summer and winter sports federations, the republican public associations representing the sports of Belarus in the international Olympic movement and the NOC regional representatives. Representatives of the NOC are employed in all regional centres of the country and the city of Minsk, under the decision of the Olympic meeting of 26 January 1993.

234. Financing of the NOC: The NOC is completely financed at the expense of independent sources. Financial assets are used to conduct sporting actions under the patronage of the IOC and the NOC of Belarus and provide for the preparation and participation of Belarusian sportspeople in the largest international competitions, including the Olympic Games.

235. The PC of Belarus: The PC of Belarus is the public organization recognized by the International and European Paralympic committees. The PC of Belarus heads the Paralympic movement of Belarus and participates in developing and implementing a uniform state policy for the promotion of physical training and sport among disabled individuals, including children with delayed development, together with the Ministry of Sports and Tourism, the Ministry of Labour and Social Protection, the Ministry of Health, the Ministry of Education and public associations for disabled people. It is guided in its activities by the legislation of Belarus, the charters of the International and European Paralympic committees and the Olympic Charter.

§2. The Association of the Belarusian Football Federation

236. The Association of the Belarusian Football Federation (ABFF) was formed on 22 December 1989 and has been a member of FIFA/UEFA since 1992/1993. The ABFF structure includes:

(1) Members of the ABFF.
(2) Agencies of the ABFF:
  (a) The decision-making authority, including the Executive Board, the Executive Board Bureau and the Chair.
  (b) The disciplinary and jurisdictional authorities, including the Football Arbitration Committee, the Appeals Committee, the Disciplinary Committee, the Committee on Club Licensing, the Appeals Committee for Club Licensing, the Committee on the Status and Transfer of Players and the Ethics Committee.
  (c) The administrative authority, including the administration of the ABFF.
  (d) The financial control body, including the Auditing Commission.
(3) Committees:
  (a) Judicial Committee.
  (b) Disciplinary Committee: The competence of the Disciplinary Committee includes:
  – consideration of the disciplinary infringements, made in the course of and communications involved in carrying out national football competitions;
  – consideration of disputes connected with infringements made in the course of and communications involved in carrying out national football competitions, including the technical (technician safety and the law and order and safety in stadiums) and disciplinary rules;
  – consideration of infringements of the disciplinary code (regulations) for associations, conducting competitions, ABFF members, judges, sportspeople, coaches, proprietors of football clubs and other workers, including in the concrete relations with football clubs, member associations;
  (c) Licensing Committee: The Licensing Committee is a directive body and the decision maker for the licensing of football clubs. It decides whether to issue a licence on the basis of the presented documents and operates in

conformity with the system of licensing of ABFF football clubs, taking into account deadlines for providing documents.

(d) Appeals Committee.

(e) Medical Board: The main objectives and commission problems of the Medical Board include:

– the medical maintenance of members of the national football teams of Belarus and clubs of the higher, first and second leagues;
– maintaining qualitative health services for all competitions in Belarus and its limits;
– developing and strengthening professional communication with the national medical committees of football federations of foreign countries.

(f) Committee of Regional Federations.

(g) Committee on Sports Constructions and the Safety Maintenance of Football Arenas. The primary goal of this committee is the conformity of sports constructions to the requirements of ABFF Management on the licensing of football clubs and the infrastructural criteria for conducting matches under the aegis of the association.

(h) Committee on Child and Youth Football.

(i) Committee on the Status and Transfer of Football Players: This committee considers the situations, infringements and requirements of the legal status of football players participating in national football competitions, the transfer of football players and the situations connected with infringements of requirements regarding the legal status of coaches (as a body of the first instance).

(j) Committee for Veterans and Mass Football: The primary goals of this committee are the popularization and development of mass and veteran football and football for disabled individuals and interactions with other domestic and international charitable organizations in deciding the given direction of regional football.

(k) Female Football Committee: This committee participates in planning the development program for female footballers in Belarus; coordinates the organization, management and conduct of football competitions for female players at the national level; and develops regulations, plans and calendars for female football competitions, as organized by the ABFF.

(4) Departments of the ABFF:

(a) Department of Organizational and Personnel Management.
(b) Department for Competition Organization.
(c) International Legal Department.
(d) Technical Department.
(e) Refereeing and Inspection Department.
(f) Financial and Economic Department.
(g) Department of Licensing.
(h) Department on Working with Mass Media.
(i) Marketing Department.
(j) Insurance Department.
(k) Department of Buildings and Structure Maintenance.

§3. Belarusian Athletics Federation

237. The public association, the Belarusian Athletics Federation (BAF) is a voluntary, independent public association created on the basis of the free association of sportspeople, coaches and experts engaged in the development and popularization of track and field athletics in Belarus.

238. The BAF has the status of a republican public association and operates in the territory of Belarus according to the Constitution of Belarus, the Law of Belarus 'On Public Associations', other legal acts of Belarus, the international treaties of Belarus, the Charter of the NOC, its own charter and the charters of the International Association of Athletics Federations (IAAF) and the European Athletic Association (EAA).

239. Citizens of Belarus, foreign citizens and persons without citizenship who are 16 years or older and residing in Belarus can be members of the BAF if they wish to take part in realizing its authorized purposes, addressing problems and recognizing the Charter and are engaged in track and field athletics or in promoting its development, by paying introductory and membership dues. Minors younger than 16 years can gain BAF membership with the written approval of their parents (or lawful representatives).

240. Sportspeople, coaches, scientists, writers, journalists, other experts, public figures and sports veterans who have been members of the BAF and have made significant contributions to the development of track and field athletics can be made honorary members of the BAF. Honorary members of the BAF have the right to participate in the work of the directing bodies of BAF without a vote.

241. Sportspeople and coaches who are members of the BAF have no right to carry on direct or indirect negotiations, to sign contracts (agreements) for the purpose of receiving monetary or material compensation for participation in international competitions, advertising, sponsorship or the use of equipment and to use the BAF name and image without the consent of the BAF.

242. Questions of exclusion and exit from the BAF are allocated to the bodies responsible for admission to the BAF or the Committees of the BAF. Exclusion from the BAF is imposed for infringements of the Charter and evading participation in the work of the BAF. The account of members is conducted by drawing up lists by the committees of BAF regional organizations, which go to the Secretary General of the BAF.

243. The BAF has regional branches. They are created by a territorial principle in the presence of not less than twenty-five members. The supreme regional body of the BAF (Minsk City) is the Conference, which is held not less than once in two years.

244. Regional branches of the BAF work under the guidance of BAF Committees. The supervising body of regional branches is the Committee for Regional Branches, which is headed by the Chair of the Committee who is selected for a period of four years.

245. Committee sessions are convoked as required but are not rarer than once in three months. Committee emergency meetings are convoked at the initiative of the Chair, the Auditor or at the request of not less than one-third of the members of the Committee.

246. BAF has the right to check the activity of corresponding subordinate elective bodies. Decisions of bodies of BAF (bodies of its organizational structures) can be appealed against in higher elective bodies. The decision of the BAF Conference can be appealed against in judicial bodies of Belarus, in the order established by the law.

247. Under a BAF Committee decision, regional branches can be allocated the rights of a legal person. The BAF Committee has the right to specify and concretize the powers of structural divisions.

248. The supreme body of the BAF is the Conference, which is convoked once in four years under the decision of the BAF Committee. An Extraordinary Conference can be called under the decision of the Chair, under the decision of the BAF Committee, at the request of not less than three regional organizations, at the request of not less than one-third of all members of the BAF and at the request of the Central Revision Committee. For a Conference convocation, the agenda and a rate of representation are issued not later than sixty days prior to the Conference.

249. A Conference is considered competent if not less than two-thirds of the selected delegates are present. Conference decisions are accepted by the voices present by a show of hands or a secret vote, as established by the Conference. Reports are created that subscribe to who is responsible for presiding over the Conference and the Secretary.

250. Elections of structures, including Committees, the Audit Commission and individual roles, including the Chair, Vice-President and Secretary General occur, as a rule, on an alternative basis by direct vote. The voting form (open or secret) is defined by the Conference. The Chair is considered as selected if they receive the votes of more than 50% of the selected delegates. There is no restriction on the number of terms. The Chair, Vice-President and Secretary General are part of the BAF Committee. The Chair of the BAF is the Chair of the BAF Committee.

251. The supervising body of the BAF is the BAF Committee, which operates within the powers defined by the present Charter. The BAF Committee is selected at the Conference, in the quantity defined by the Conference. Committee sessions occur not less than once in six months. The Committee makes a decision by majority if not less than two-thirds of its members are present at a voting session. When equal votes are received for both sides, a decision is considered accepted by the vote of the Chair.

252. The Chair of the BAF is included in the Committee and the BAF Executive Committee structure and supervises the activity of the BAF according to the Charter. When the Chair is absent, the relevant duties pass on to the Vice-President; in their absence, the duties pass on to the Secretary General.

253. For operative decisions on organizational and executive character and financial and economic activity, the BAF Committee creates an Executive Committee. The number of members is defined by the BAF Committee. The Chair, their assistant, the Secretary General and the Chief Executive must be part of the Executive Committee.

254. The Executive Committee supervises the BAF during the period between Committee sessions, organizes voting on decisions at Conference and Committee meetings, puts into practice programmes addressing authorized BAF areas in relation to the rights and powers given by the BAF Committee and confirms positions on the payment of executive management.

255. Executive Committee sessions occur as required, but not rarer than three times in a month. The organization of Executive Committee activities is provided by the Vice-President of the BAF. The Chief Executive is appointed to the Executive Committee.

256. The Chief Executive is guided by the legislation of Belarus, the present Charter, decisions on the control of the BAF and the instructions of the BAF Chair, Vice-President and Secretary General. Decisions of the Chief Executive can be appealed against in Executive Committee meetings.

§4. Belarus Canoe Association

257. The Belarus Canoe Association (BAC) was formed on 9 September 1999. It is a non-commercial organization created on the basis of a voluntary association of sportspeople, coaches, officiators and experts in rowing, canoeing and white-water canoeing and kayaking, as well as professors, high school students, students of higher education institutes and other citizens engaged in developing and popularizing canoeing in Belarus.

258. The association is a unique organization representing Belarusian canoeing as a sport in Belarus and abroad. All canoeing competitions within the territory of Belarus occur under the aegis of the BAC. The association has the right to delegate powers for conducting national competitions.

259. The association possesses a higher jurisdiction concerning BAC members within the limits of canoeing management. The association recognizes the principles, purposes and problems of the international Olympic movement and carries out activities in interaction with the NOC and the Ministry of Sports and Tourism.

260. The association has rights given to it by its Charter and regulations, as well as decisions accepted on the basis of these documents. The association is obliged to observe the game rules accepted by the International Canoe Federation (ICF) and bears financial responsibilities to the ICF under its obligations.

261. The association holds responsibility for all property on which, under the legislation, penalties can be imposed. Founders and members of the BAC do not answer for BAC obligations and the BAC does not answer for the obligations of the founders and members. The association does not bear responsibility under state obligations and the state does not answer for the obligations of the BAC.

262. The incomes received from economic activities are not subject to distribution between members of the BAC and are used to achieve the purposes specified in the BAC Charter. The BAC property is the association property. The association bears responsibility for any property belonging to it.

263. Members (participants) of the BAC include any citizen of Belarus or any person without citizenship over the age of 16. Admission to the BAC is carried out via a written application to an acceded person of a particular governing body of an organizational division or Committee of the BAC.

264. Membership to the BAC is voluntary. Under Division IV of the Charter, a BAC member has a set of rights and obligations.

265. BAC members have the right to elect and to be elected to any organ of the association, the right to participate in all BAC events, the right to make a proposal to any BAC organ on any issue connected with BAC activity, the right to take part in the management of any BAC organ in an advisory capacity, to resort to the BAC on the defence of rights and legal interests and the right to stop being a member of the BAC.

266. The obligations of a BAC member include compliance with the requirements of the Charter, reinforcement of BAC authority, participation in BAC events, carrying out the decisions of BAC-elected organs and payment of membership fees.

267. Membership to the BAC is ended in the following cases:

(1) withdrawal from the BAC at the member's free will;
(2) exclusion from the BAC on the grounds of flagrant violation of the Charter; and
(3) regular avoidance of participation in BAC events.

268. The Charter includes the possibility to appeal an exclusion and registration. Such an appeal shall be filed within one month and shall be directed to a superior organ of the BAC. Filing of a complaint suspends an adopted decision.

269. The BAC is organized in accordance with the territorial principle. The basic BAC units are primary organizations (sections and clubs). For the establishment of a primary organization, there must be five members. The members of a primary organization elect their Chair for a two-year period.

270. Primary organizations form the city and regional organizations (federations). The supreme body of the regional and Minsk City organizations and other BAC divisions is a meeting held once every two years. The meeting is duly constituted when more than half of its members are present. The decisions are taken by a simple majority. In between meetings, the management of city and regional organizations is carried out by the Managing Board, which consists of three members. Their meetings are held as and when necessary, but not less than once in six months. The city and regional organizations have an auditor who carries out an audit once a year.

271. The BAC supreme body is the Conference held once every four years. An unscheduled Conference is formed at the request of two-thirds of BAC members or upon an initiative of the Committee or the Revision Committee.

272. The Conference is authorized to make decisions when two-thirds of elected deputies are present. The forms and conditions for voting are established by the Conference.

273. The association governing bodies are:

(1) the Conference, Executive Committee and Chair;
(2) the auditing body is the Revision Committee or the Auditor.

274. The Committee, the Revision Committee, the BAC Chair and two representatives (one of which is the Executive Director) are elected by the Conference.

275. The Committee is a governing body of the association elected for four years. The Committee is responsible for the programme, budget, property, referee commissions, clubs, sections and the establishment and liquidation of commercial organizations. It elects from its members the Secretary and the Executive Committee and delegates a part of its authority to these bodies.

276. The BAC Chair is also the Chair of the BAC Committee and represents the BAC in state organs and in non-governmental organizations. The Chair is elected at the Conference for four years.

277. The main obligations of the Chair are:

– decisions on credits;
– supervision of BAC Committee work;
– hiring and laying off salaried employees.

278. The Executive Committee is elected for organizational, financial and economical objects. The number of Executive Committee members is established by the Committee. The Executive Director is the representative of the Chair and supervises the Executive Committee's work.

279. The Executive Committee meeting is held once every three months. The meeting is duly formed when more than half of its members are present. The decisions of the Executive Committee are taken by the simple majority of members present at the meeting.

280. The Revision Committee is governed by its Chair, elected from the Revision Committee's members. The Revision Committee controls the BAC's compliance with Belarusian legislation and the BAC Charter and carries out the decisions of the Conference and Committee.

281. The Revision Committee controls the timeliness and good reasoning of answers to applications, letters and complaints. The Revision Committee's members take part in the work of BAC-elected organs with advisory rights.

282. The Revision Committee carries out audits as and when necessary, but not less than once a year. A meeting of the Revision Committee is duly held when more than half of its members are present. The decisions of the Revision Committee are taken by a simple majority. The membership requirements for joining the Revision Committee are obligatory for all its members. The Revision Committee is placed under the responsibility of the Conference.

283. The members of the Revision Committee cannot be elected to other BAC organs and cannot be Chair of any established self-sustaining divisions.

284. The decision of the BAC organs and its officials can be appealed to the Revision Committee; decisions of the Revision Committee can be appealed to the Conference.

§5. Belarusian Basketball Federation

285. On 10 July 1992, the Executive Committee of the International Basketball Federation (FIBA) accepted the Belarusian national basketball association as FIBA member. On 11 January 1994, the public association, the Belarusian Basketball Federation (BBF), was registered by the NOC of Belarus and in 1997 by the Ministry of Justice of Belarus.

286. The BBF is a voluntary association of citizens. The BBF is a republican public association that conducts activities in all territories of Belarus, has organizational structures created on territorial principles and operates on the basis of a Charter.

287. The BBF carries out activities according to the rules of FIBA and the International Federation of Basketball in Europe (FIBA-EUROPE).

288. A member of the BBF can be:

(1) Citizens of Belarus, as a rule, who are 14 years or older and interested in contributing to the decisions of the BBF, being basketball players, coaches or judges, or are other citizens supporting the purposes and problems of the BBF. Citizens between 14 and 16 years of age can be members of the BBF with written approval from their lawful representatives.
(2) Foreign citizens and persons without citizenship can be BBF members, except for cases established by law or the international contracts of Belarus.

289. Admission to BBF membership is the responsibility of the BBF Executive Committee and the boards of its organizational structures on the basis of the individual written statements of citizens.

290. The status of a BBF member can be removed by the decision of the Executive Committee or the boards of organizational structures responsible for membership and entrance fee payments. These boards are obliged to notify the BBF Executive Committee in writing within a month of accepting new BBF members.

291. The supreme body of the BBF is the BBF Conference, over which the Chair presides. The Conference occurs once every four years. An Extraordinary Conference can be called at the request of the Chair, the Revision Committee or at the written request of more than half the members of the BBF. The election of delegates to the Conference and their powers are defined according to the regulations for conducting Conferences and the confirmed Chair.

292. During the period between Conferences, management of activity is carried out by the BBF Committee. The quantitative structure of the Committee is defined by the Conference. The Committee structure includes ex officio:

(1) the Chair of the BBF;
(2) the first assistants – the Secretary General and the Vice-Presidents of the BBF;
(3) the chairs of regional branch boards;
(4) the state coaches and main coaches of the male and female national teams and the Chair of the Coach's Council;
(5) other persons selected by the Conference.

293. For operative decisions on the current activities of the BBF Committee, the BBF selects an Executive Committee. The Executive Committee includes the Chair or a first assistant (the Secretary General).

294. The quantity of members of the Executive Committee is defined by the Committee. In the structure of the Executive Committee are the Chair, the First Assistant – Secretary General – Vice-Presidents, the Chief Executive, the State Coach and other members selected by the Committee.

295. The Executive Committee creates other commissions, the Board of Guardians and other councils for the direction of BBF activities. The Board of Guardians is headed by the Chair of the Trustee Council and is selected from council members. The Board of Guardians unites the heads of legal bodies, other organizations and individuals, such as businesspeople supporting the BBF voluntarily, due to general interest in its purposes and problems.

296. The list of created bureaus, commissions and councils is confirmed by the Executive Committee of the BBF. The chairs of these bodies are selected at their meetings. Positions in commissions and councils should correspond to the present Charter and be affirmed by the Executive Committee. The Executive Committee considers and accepts joint decisions on questions arriving from state bodies and FIBA, holding the final decision power.

297. The Chair of the BBF is selected via election at a Conference from among BBF members. Any BBF member can offer a nominee for the post of Chair.

298. Current organizational, financial and economic activity carried out by the BBF occurs under the management of the Chief Executive. The functional duties of the Chief Executive are affirmed by the Chair.

299. The control body of the BBF is the Revision Committee. The Revision Committee carries out checks on the initiatives or instructions of the Conference or the Committee. Members of the Revision Committee have the right to demand from the BBF officials documents and personal explanations necessary for their work. The Revision Committee is a check to the Committee and Conferences. Members of the Revision Committee cannot be members of the Executive Committee, the Committee or hold any other post within the BBF.

300. Decisions of BBF bodies, including parts of the organizational structure of the BBF, can be appealed to the corresponding control or to a higher body in the BBF.

301. The organizational structure of the BBF includes regional branches (hereinafter 'branches') and primary organizations. Branches are created in every area, including the city of Minsk. A branch is created with not less than ten members of the BBF.

302. Decisions on the creation and termination of branches are accepted by the Executive Committee. Under the decision of the Committee, branches can be allocated the rights of a legal person and be registered with the enforcement authorities according to the order established in legislation.

303. Primary organizations are the associations of citizens created at their place of work, study or residence. Primary organizations can be created with the presence of not less than three persons. Decisions on the establishment of primary organizations are made by a general meeting of a regional branch where such primary organization is to be established. Primary organizations are part of the BBF.

§6. Belarusian Gymnastics Association

304. The public organization, the Belarusian Gymnastics Association (BGA) was formed on 14 September 1993. The BGA was officially recognized by the International Federation of Gymnastics (IFG) and the European Union of Gymnastics (UEG) in 1993 as a unique organization possessing special powers for the management and development of gymnastics, for carrying out national and international competitions in the territory of Belarus, for representing all types of gymnastics in international sport relations and for communicating with the IFG, the UEG, national gymnastics federations in other countries and other foreign, Belarusian and international associations.

305. The structure of the BGA includes:

(1) The Technical Committee on Male Gymnastics
(2) The Technical Committee on Female Gymnastics
(3) The Technical Committee on Artistic Gymnastics
(4) The Technical Committee on Trampolining
(5) The Belarusian Federation of Acrobatics
(6) The Technical Committee on Aerobics
(7) The Medical and Anti-doping Commission.

306. The BGA is a voluntary, independent organization created on the basis of the public and free association of sportspeople, coaches, judges and experts on gymnastics, aerobics, acrobatics and trampolining, as well as citizens engaged in the development and popularization of these sports in Belarus.

307. The supreme body of the BGA is the Conference, which is convoked once every four years. During the period between Conferences, the management of BGA activity is conducted by the supervising body – the Committee.

308. The executive office of the BGA is the Executive Bureau. The Chair, Vice-Presidents and the Secretary General are part of the Executive Bureau. The Revision Committee is the controlling body of the BGA. The Revision Committee maintains control over the BGA's financial and economic activities.

309. The organizational structure of the BGA includes:

(1) Local organizations – gymnastics federations in places that are registered within the territory of regions (including Minsk) and containing not less than three members.

310. Citizens of Belarus, foreign citizens and persons without citizenship, who are 16 years or older (those under 16 must have the written permission of their lawful guardians) and are engaged in gymnastics, aerobics, acrobatics or trampolining can be BGA members, on recognizing the Charter of the BGA, participating in its decision making and paying membership dues.

Part II. Sports and Status

Chapter 1. Public Regulations

§1. Qualification of Legal Status

311. The sportsperson is the physical person who is regularly engaged in sport and takes part in sports competitions. The sportsperson and the coach, in the overwhelming majority of cases, are hired workers, to whom the norms of the labour legislation extend. However, the legislation does not exclude the registration of the sportsperson (or coach or referee) as an individual businessperson and the rendering of sporting 'services' by them to the relevant club or federation.

§2. Employment and Labour Market Regulations

I. General Rules

312. Article 319 of the LC states that the regulations for the working conditions of physical training and sports organization employees and the sportspeople and coaches of national teams of the Republic of Belarus are determined by the republic body of the state. This republic body conducts the state policy in the field of physical culture and sport, taking into account the norms established by the present Code. Work for sportspeople is regulated by Chapter 26-1 of the LC.

313. In accordance with Article 55 of the LPCS, professional sports are the com mercial, labour and other activities not forbidden by legislation directed towards the achievement of high sports results and the receipt of income (compensation) for the organization of and (or) participation in sporting events. The relations arising in professional sports are regulated by the CC of Belarus, the LC, the LPCS and other legislative acts.

II. Social Dialogue

314. The social dialogue in sport refers to section IV of the LC, 'The General Regulations of Collective Labour Relations'. In the legislation of Belarus, the term 'social partnership' is used. The LC explains the norms of social partnership in Chapter 33 'General Provisions on Social Partnership', Chapter 34 'Collective

Negotiations' and Chapter 35 'Agreements, Collective Agreements'. Considering the absence of sport specificity in the given norms, an examination of the section of the encyclopaedia devoted to the regulation of the labour laws of Belarus is recommended.

III. Rules on Salaries Paid by the State

315. The resolution of the Ministry of Sport and Tourism dated 30 December 2019, No. 48[67] 'On the special features of the regulation of the work of employees engaged in educational activities in the field of physical culture and sport' regulates orders on the payment of workers in the sphere of sport and sports formation, financed at the expense of the state budget Decision No. 48 establishes the method and order of rates (salaries) for workers in these organizations, the rules for organizations on the payment of coach-teachers and coaches, the requirements for training process modes and enrolment in educational and sports groups, the rates (salary) for separate heads and experts and the rates for teaching work.

In the Republic of Belarus, employees of budget organizations engaged in pedagogical activities in the field of physical culture and sports are entitled to receive incentive payments. This issue is regulated by the resolution of the Ministry of Sport and Tourism dated 24 July 2019, No. 33[68] 'On the Remuneration of Employees in the Field of Physical Culture, Sports and Tourism' (updated version: 13 July 2021). This resolution defines the tariff categories for the positions of employees, the list of incentive payments, as well as the procedure for implementing and the amount of such payments.

In order to stimulate the achievement of high sports results, personal scholarships are paid in the Republic of Belarus. The procedure, amounts and conditions for the payment of personal scholarships are determined by the Decree of the President of the Republic of Belarus No. 190 of 15.04.2013 (ed. of 09.09.2019) 'On measures to stimulate the achievement of high sports results' (hereinafter 'Decree No. 190').[69] In addition, in accordance with paragraph 3 of Decree No. 190, some categories of athletes (who won medals at international competitions, set records or won (drew) in the match of the final tournament of the Olympic Games, World and European championships, world and European cups as part of teams in game sports, in the world group match of the Davis Cup and the Fed Cup (tennis) have the right to receive prizes in cash or in kind. Coaches who have participated in the sports training of such athletes also are entitled to receive remuneration in the amount of 20 to 100 per cent of the prize value, depending on the degree of participation in the sports training.

Decree of the President of the Republic of Belarus No. 329 dated 9 September 2019 'On National and United Teams of the Republic of Belarus in Sports'[70] (hereinafter 'Decree No. 329') regulates the issues of concluding employment contracts

67. The National Register of Legal Acts of Belarus, 22 Jan. 2020, No. 8/35016.
68. The National Register of Legal Acts of Belarus, 14 Aug. 2019, No. 8/34464.
69. The National Register of Legal Acts of Belarus, 18 Apr. 2013, No. 1/14217.
70. The National Register of Legal Acts of Belarus, 11 Sep. 2019, No. 1/18554.

and wages of persons who are members of national and united teams of the Republic of Belarus. In accordance with paragraph 11 of Decree No. 329, the Ministry of Sports and Tourism is authorized to conclude and terminate employment contracts with athletes, coaches and other specialists who are part of the staff of national teams. In turn, the Ministry shall conclude civil law contracts with sports athletes of united teams, military personnel and athletes of national teams who are not part of the staff. In addition, in accordance with paragraph 6 of the Decree, military personnel who are enrolled in national teams are not deprived of their rights, guarantees, compensation and provision with money, allowances and other property that they are entitled to in accordance with the law.

The issues of payment of scholarships to athletes of national and united teams are regulated by Resolution of the Council of Ministers of the Republic of Belarus of 12.07.2018 N 528 (updated version: 30.04.2019) 'On approval of the Regulations on the Procedure for Payment and Amounts of Scholarships to Athletes of National and United Teams of the Republic of Belarus in Sports, Sports Reserve at the Expense of Local Budgets'[71] (hereinafter 'Resolution No. 528'). In accordance with paragraph 4 of Resolution No. 528, these scholarships are paid by local executive and administrative bodies based on the decisions of the relevant local Councils of Deputies. In addition, the maximum amounts of scholarships paid to athletes at the expense of local budgets for the achieved sports results are set out in the Annex to Resolution No. 528.

316. The contract is the labour contract concluded in writing for the term defined in it, containing features in agreement with the general norms of the legislation on work and providing concrete minimum indemnification for the deterioration of the legal status of a sportsperson-instructor or a coach of a national sporting team of Belarus.

317. The contract is concluded between the Ministry of Sports and Tourism of Belarus (hereinafter 'the employer') and a sportsperson-instructor or a coach of a national team of Belarus (hereinafter 'the worker') at the commencement of the working period.

318. The contract is concluded in writing in two copies for the term of not less than one year. The concrete terms of the contract are defined by the agreement of both parties. The validity period of the contract is defined as follows:

(1) for a working woman on maternity leave or a mother (or the father of the child instead of mother, the trustee) on parental leave not less than before the termination of the specified leave;
(2) for an employee who conscientiously works and does not violate the norms of labour, performance and technological discipline and who is no more than two years before retirement – not less than before the reaching of the stated age.

71. The National Register of Legal Acts of Belarus, 14 Jul. 2018, No. 5/45384.

319. The employer, with the consent of the mother (or the father of the child instead of the mother, the trustee) who has started to work before or after their parental leave termination, before the child reaches the age of three, is obliged to prolong the contract for a term of not less than before the child reaches the age of five.

320. The contract is signed by the employer and the worker and is stored by each of the parties. The contract is the basis for the appointment order. The contract comes into force from the date of its signing or another date specified within it.

321. In the contract, the following conditions should be specified as obligatory:

(1) Signing date.
(2) Workplace.
(3) The worker's post.
(4) The valid contract period.
(5) The rights of the parties, including the right of the employer, to:
 (a) Reduce (deprive) awards of all kinds, irrespective of the worker's disciplinary responsibility, for:
  (i) absence from a workplace without a good reason;
  (ii) untimely performance or default of labour duties without a valid excuse;
  (iii) use of state property not for the designed purpose.
 (b) Reduce the worker's holidays in the corresponding year for a number of days of deliberate default of labour duties by the worker for more than three hours within the working day, without valid excuse. Thus, holidays should be not less than twenty-four calendar days.
(6) The duties and responsibilities of the parties include:
 (a) The duty of each party that has concluded the contract, not later than one month before the expiry of the term of action of the contract, to warn the other party in writing about the decision to continue or stop labour relations.
 (b) Full liability for damage caused to the employer because of the worker receiving excessive monetary payments (except for cases of calculation errors), providing the wrong account information.
 (c) Conditions of the organization and payment of the worker (taking into account the results of their work), dependent on the measures of encouragement on observance of the rules of the internal labour schedule.
(7) Additional measures of stimulation of work, including:
 (a) Granting to the worker additional incentive holidays, with the preservation of wages, of five calendar days.
 (b) Increasing the official salary (no more than 50% if a larger amount is not provided for by the legislation).
 (c) The size of the minimum indemnification for deterioration of the legal status of the worker, as established by the legislation.

322. The parties can provide in the contract:

(1) Labour and social privileges and guarantees to workers.
(2) Additional conditions that do not worsen the position of the worker in comparison with the legislation.
(3) Change of contract conditions is made, when due hereunder, at the agreement of all parties or on the basis provided for by the legislation.

323. The contract terminates on:

(1) the expiration of its term;
(2) the infringement of rules for labour safety and safety precautions or the entailed mutilation or death of another worker;
(3) the causing of property damage, in connection with the execution of labour duties, to the state and legal and (or) physical persons, as established by a decision deemed valid by a court or a decision on administrative responsibility accepted by an authorized state body (official);
(4) drinking of spirits or the use of narcotics or toxins in working hours or in the workplace;
(5) non-provision of appropriate labour discipline to subordinates, concealment of the infringement of labour discipline by them or non-involvement without a valid excuse; a person is deemed guilty via the responsibility established by the legislation for such infringements;
(6) any other basis provided by the legislation on work.

324. The contract can be terminated early:

(1) At the initiative of the employer on the additional basis provided for by the legislation, following worker infringements of the labour duties assigned to them.
(2) Numerous (two or more times within six months) transfers of incomplete or doubtful data to authorized bodies.
(3) Non-acceptance, without a valid excuse established by the lawful instructions of law-enforcement or control bodies, of measures for eliminating revealed infringements and also of compensation owed for the material damage caused to the state as a result of infringing the current legislation.
(4) On the request of the worker in case of default or inadequate performance because of the conditions of the contract.

325. The contract can be prolonged within the maximum term of its action (Article 17(2) LC) by the agreement of the parties for a term of not less than one year. For a smaller term, the contract lasts from the written approval of the worker if another date is not established by the President of Belarus.

326. The contract with a pregnant woman lasts from her consent through pregnancy or until another term by the agreement of both parties.

327. After the maximum period of contract validity, and also in cases of the transfer of workers to other workplaces, by the arrangement of both parties, the new contract is valid for a term of not less than one year.

328. If, after the expiry of the term of the contract, labour relations proceed and any of the parties has not demanded their termination, the contract will be transformed into a labour contract concluded for an uncertain term.

§3. Social Security

I. Pension Plan

329. The provision of pensions, including for sportspeople, is regulated by the Law of Belarus dated 17 April 1992, No. 1596-XII (updated version: 29 December 2020) 'On the Provision of Pensions'.[72] Article 49-2 of the specified law 'Conditions for the Appointment of Pensions to Sportspeople' establishes that sportspeople have the right to a long-service pension under the following circumstances:

(1) for men with work experience of no less than 25 years, of which 15 years are professional sports activity;
(2) for women with work experience of no less than 20 years, of which 10 years are professional sports activity.

330. Sportspeople who were members of a national team of Belarus for not less than five years have the right to a long-service pension with work experience of not less than 25 years for men and 20 years for women. The list of categories of sportspeople, as approved by the decision of the Council of Ministers of Belarus on 1 April 1994, No. 205 'About the Statement of the List of Categories of Sportspeople with the Right to a Long-Service Pension under the Condition of Time in a National Team of Belarus of Not Less of Five Years'[73] includes:

(1) Winners of Olympic Games.
(2) World and European Champions.
(3) Prize-winners of the World and European Championships.
(4) Winners of World and European Cups.
(5) Prize-winners of World and European Cups.
(6) Winners of the European Cup tournaments in game types of sport.
(7) The deserved 'masters of sport' of Belarus (the deserved 'masters of sport' of the former USSR).
(8) 'Masters of sport of Belarus of the international class' ('masters of sport of the former USSR' of the international class).
(9) International grandmasters.

---

72. Viedamasci Viarchounaha Savieta Respubliki Belarus', 15 Jun. 1992, No. 17, Art. 275.
73. Collection of Regulations of Government of Republic of Belarus, 1994, No. 10, Art. 164.

331. Sportspeople for whom professional pension insurance was paid have the right to pre-schedule a professional pension (before a generally established pension age) and the additional professional pension paid during the period after a sportsperson reaches a generally established pension age. It is thus defined that if the worker continues to work (or renews work during the period when the pre-scheduled professional pension is paid to them) at a workplace included in the list of workplaces with special working conditions, the payment of the pre-scheduled professional pension for work in such conditions stops.

II. Professional Pension Insurance

332. The legal basis, the principles of organization, the function of professional pension insurance and the definition of the rights and duties of the subjects of professional pension insurance was established in the Law of Belarus from 5 January 2008, No. 322-Z (updated version: 10 December 2020) 'On Professional Pension Insurance'[74] (hereinafter 'the Law on Pension Insurance').

333. According to the Law on Pension Insurance, insurers by type of insurance are workers employed in special working conditions under labour contracts, making payments to professional pension insurance. An employer, with trade union participation, makes the local rules and confirms the internal list of workplaces with special working conditions (payments of professional pension insurance are paid for workers in workplaces included in the list with special working conditions).

334. Categories of the workers subject to professional pension insurance are specified in Article 5 of the law. In one case, concrete roles, trades, works and manufacturers are named; in others, instructions on the lists contain the decision of the Council of Ministers of Belarus dated 9 October 2008, No. 1490 'About Some Questions of Professional Pension Insurance' (updated version: 24 June 2016)[75] (hereinafter 'Decision No. 1490'). So, the sportspeople occupied with the following types of sport are subject to professional pension insurance: acrobatics, badminton, basketball, biathlon, boxing, Greco-Roman wrestling, cycling, water polo, water skiing, volleyball, handball, gymnastic sports, artistic gymnastics, mountain skiing, academic rowing, rowing on kayaks and canoes, judo, karate, kickboxing, sport skating, equestrian sports, track and field athletics, biathlons, cross-countries, motoball, motorcycle sport, parachuting, sailing, swimming, synchronized swimming, diving, trampolining, sambo-wrestling, high-speed swimming in flippers, snowboarding, modern pentathlon, archery, shooting, Thai boxing, taekwondo, tennis, table tennis, triathlons, weightlifting, wushu, fencing, figure skating, freestyle skating, football, hockey, field hockey, short-track speed skating.

---

74. The National Register of Legal Acts of Belarus, 21 Jan. 2008, No. 16, 2/1419.
75. The National Register of Legal Acts of Belarus, 20 Oct. 2008, No. 249, 5/28508.

335. The employer makes an estimation of working conditions and the features of work in designated workplaces via the application of criteria for estimating working conditions.

336. For sportspeople engaged in professional sports who are also members of a national sporting team of Belarus, the criteria for estimating working conditions are:

(1) Inclusion in the structure of a national sports team of Belarus.
(2) The conclusion of an employment agreement with the Ministry of Sports and Tourism, Olympic training centre, centre for Olympic reserves, republican state-public association or volunteer society of assistance of army, aircraft and the fleet of Belarus.
(3) Achievement of one of the following sports results, confirmed with official reports of competitions:
  (a) In Olympic sports:
    (i) first to sixth places in the Olympic Games;
    (ii) first to third places in the World Championships;
    (iii) first place or, twice within four years, second and (or) third places in the European Championships;
    (iv) first to third places at World Cup competitions;
    (v) first to third places at a Grand Slam, the Davis Cup or the Federation Cup for tennis.
  (b) In non-Olympic sports:
    (i) first place in the World Championships;
    (ii) first place at World Cup competitions;
    (iii) first place at the European Championships for motoball.

337. Concerning the sportspeople who are engaged in professional sport, the criteria for estimating working conditions include:

(1) Concluding an employment agreement with the Ministry of Sports and Tourism, a state body exercising administration according to its competence in the sphere of physical training and sport or the physical training and sports organization.
(2) Direct employment in a professional sports activity listed as eligible for professional pension, confirmed by Decision No. 1490.

338. Applying the established criteria for estimating the working conditions of professional sports activity involves the type of labour activity aimed at the achievement of high sports results and consistency in preparing for sports competitions and participation in them by means of a combination of training and competitive activity. Professional sports activity assumes regular employment by the selected type of sport as a principal activity, labour relations with the state body exercising administration in the sphere of physical training and sport, the physical training and sports organization and the receipt of earnings (payment) for realization of the specified activity.

339. Estimating the working conditions of the sportspeople engaged in professional sport for professional pension insurance, along with the above-stated criteria, involves analysing their direct employment by professional sports activity, as a principal kind of activity should not be less than the full rate considered (similar employment conditions on the full rate is established for all other persons provided in Article 5 of the Law on Pension Insurance).

340. Professional pension insurance for workers occupied in the workplaces included in the list of special working conditions of the organization is carried out during the periods of their direct labour activity at these workplaces and on labour holidays.

341. If the results of the subsequent estimation of working conditions for a certain workplace find that the factors used are not established or confirmed, the basis for the inclusion in the list of workplaces with special working conditions is subject to an exception of the specified list.

342. Payments of professional pension insurance are made as established by the Decree of the President of Belarus dated 10 January 2009, No. 23 (updated version: 17 January 2020) 'On Tariffs of Payments for Professional Pension Insurance'[76] in relation to tariffs. An order of the Ministry of Labour and Social Protection and the confirmed Decree of the President of Belarus dated 16 January 2009, No. 40 (updated version: 10 February 2020, No. 48)[77] (hereinafter 'Rule No. 40') provides rules on obligatory insurance payments, payments of professional pension insurance and other payments for the social protection of the population.

343. Accidents during sports competitions or preparation for competitions that are directly connected with the professional work of sportspeople and the coaches engaged on the basis of labour contracts (agreements), irrespective of the quantity of victims and the weight of the damages to health received by them, are investigated by the employer and the insurer, with the participation of the authorized representative of the trade union (or other representative body of the specified workers). Results of the investigation are provided by a certificate on the accident on workplace form H-1 PS. (Article 36-1, approved by the decision of the Council of Ministers 18 January 2007, No. 60[78]).

§4. Dispute Settlement

344. Article 4 of the LC regulates labour relations based on the labour contract, as well as relations connected with labour disputes. Consideration of labour disputes, including the participation of sportspeople, is regulated by Chapter 17 'The

76. The National Register of Legal Acts of Belarus, 19 Jan. 2009, No. 14, 1/10382.
77. The National Register of Legal Acts of Belarus, 22 Jan. 2009, No. 17, 1/10419.
78. The National Register of Legal Acts of Belarus, 25 Jan. 2007, No. 18, 5/24578.

Resolution of Individual Labour Disputes' and Chapter 36 'The Resolution of Collective Labour Disputes'. Due to the absence of features for considering labour disputes with sportspeople, examining the corresponding section of the encyclopaedia about the labour law of Belarus is recommended.

Chapter 2. Private Regulations

§1. FOOTBALL

345. The most regulated status of the sportsperson is in football (soccer). The document regulating the status and transfer of professional football players is the Regulations of the Associations of the BFF. The given regulations have operated since 2006 in relation to rules for the transfer of football players and the admission (registration) of football players to competitions operating under the aegis of the ABFF.

I. Status of Football Players

346. The football players participating in competitions under the aegis of the BFF are either amateurs or professionals. The football player receives the status of professional from the moment of the conclusion of a contract with a professional football club for participating in competitions.

347. Professional football players are players who have a written contract with their club and receive an income over the indemnification of their expenses for their football activity. Activities of the professional football player are regulated by the current legislation of Belarus and the authorized documents and regulations of FIFA, UEFA and the BFF.

348. Football players who do not receive any compensation, besides indemnification of actual expenses (payment for food, travel, accommodation, equipment, insurance) connected with the preparation for and participation in competitions or in connection with other activities concerning the preparation for and participation in competitions are considered amateurs.

349. Football players registered as professionals can change their status to amateur by submitting to the BFF a corresponding written statement, thirty days after the last official match in which they took part as a professional has been entered into the minutes.

350. For football players with amateur status, indemnification for preparation and training is not paid. However, if the football player, within thirty months from the moment of acquiring the status of amateur, receives the status of professional, their new club pays indemnification for preparation and training.

351. Any conflict concerning the transition of football players and the definition of the status of football players is under the competence of the Committee for Players' Status.

II. Registration for Competition

352. Clubs wishing to involve a football player in competitions should register the player with the relevant association according to conditions defined by the regulations. Football players who have not been registered with the BFF may not participate in competitions. The certificate for player registration is issued according to authorized documents and the regulations of FIFA, UEFA and the BFF.

353. A football player can be registered for performance in competitions for only one club. For one season, registration of the football player is limited, as a rule, to one transfer. The second transfer and registration of the football player are authorized only in the cases mentioned below:

(1) Transfer of the football player by mutual consent of three parties (the two clubs and the football player).
(2) Granting the football player the status of 'free agent' under a corresponding decision of the Committee, but no more than two times per season.
(3) Return of the football player to a former club after the expiration of the valid period for transfer within the transfer contract for a 'rented' football player and, equally, the transfer of such players to other clubs on the terms of 'rent' if the clubs and the player agree to this transfer.
(4) Exclusion of clubs from competitions.

354. In all cases, during one season, a football player can be registered (declared) for participation in a competition for no more than two clubs.

355. An amateur football player, when signing a professional contract with a club, can be declared for this club outside of the terms of the registration period.

356. If a football player's contract has expired before the termination of the registration period and the player signs a new contract, the club accepting such a football player has the right to declare it outside of the terms of the registration period.

357. A club or football school should create a football passport for each football player over 12 years of age, which reflects the career of this football player in chronological order. Thus, the club or football school should keep an account of all football players from 8 years of age.

358. Associations include football players in competitions only in the presence of a team application form that includes the passport of each player on the team.

359. Football players moving to a Belarusian football club from a foreign football club can be registered in the relevant association only after receipt of the FIFA International Transfer Certificate (FITC) from the foreign football association to which the former club of this player belongs, according to FIFA Regulations on the status and transfer of football players. A FITC is not required for football players of 12 years and under.

III. Professional Football Players

360. Each football player registered by the BFF as a professional is obliged to have a written contract with their employing club, for a term of up to five years. The contract, and all appendices, changes and additions, should be made in writing, signed page by page by the parties, be assured by the stamp of the club and be presented by the club in three copies for the player's registration with the relevant association.

361. A contract between a football club and a football player between the age of 14 and 18 is allowed only with the notarized consent of one of the player's parents or guardians. Thus, the term of such a contract cannot exceed three years.

362. The basis for refusing to register a contract and the appendices, changes and additions to it, is non-observance by the parties of the requirements of the contract, according to the present Regulations, the current legislation of Belarus and the authorized documents and regulations of FIFA, UEFA and the BFF.

363. The contract should provide without fail:

(1) The surname, first name, date of birth and nationality of the football player and the full name of the professional football club with indication of the legal format.
(2) Information on the identity documents of the professional football player.
(3) Information on the representative of the football club who has signed the contract and the basis by virtue of which the representative is endowed with the appropriate authority;
(4) The place and date of conclusion of the contract.
(5) The employment start date and duration of the contract.
(6) The payment conditions for the activities of the professional football player (including wages, additional payments, bonuses and incentive payments).
(7) The working hours and time off from work.
(8) The obligation of the football club to provide the professional football player with mandatory social insurance, in accordance with labour and other laws of the Republic of Belarus.
(9) The obligation of the football club to provide the professional football player with life and health insurance, as well as medical care insurance, to provide the professional football player with additional medical and other services in excess of the programmes of compulsory health insurance, with an indication of the conditions of these types of insurance.
(10) The obligation of the football club to organize, at its expense, mandatory preliminary and annual periodic medical examination of a professional football player and extraordinary medical examinations of a professional football player at their request in accordance with medical recommendations, as well as the obligation of a professional football player to pass these medical examinations and follow medical recommendations.

(11) The obligation of the football club to provide training activities and opportunities for the professional football player to participate in sports competitions.
(12) The obligation of the football club to provide the professional football player with necessary professional sports equipment and inventory and other necessary means for carrying out their activities, and the obligation to maintain the equipment in useable conditions.
(13) The obligation of the football club, in the period of recovery time required by the professional football player due to a sports injury received in the performance of their duties under the contract, at its own expense, to make extra temporary disability benefit payments to the player to the level of medium-sized earnings, in cases where the size of the allowance is below the average earnings of a professional footballer and the difference between the size of the allowance and the amount of average earnings is not covered by payments from the insurance taken by the football club.
(14) The obligation of the professional football player to comply with the sports regime established by the football club and to execute preparation plans for sports competitions.
(15) The obligation of the professional football player to participate in sports events only at the direction of the football club.
(16) The obligation of the professional football player to not use prohibited means of improvement (doping) and (or) methods of passing doping control.
(17) The consent of the professional football player to transfer their personal data and a copy of their contract with the football club to the BFF.
(18) The unconditional obligation of the parties to comply with the statutes and governing documents of FIFA, UEFA and the BFF.
(19) Reference to the use (or non-use) of agent services in the drafting of the contract.

364. The order of payment by the club to the football player of awards, surcharges, extra charges, grants, material aid and other kinds of compensation, as well as the granting of other privileges of a material character, is established according to the current legislation and can be provided for directly in the text of the contract or in the local statutory act of the club or in a special addition (appendix) to the contract. Presence of such an addition (appendix) should be reflected in the contract text. Registration of the given appendix with the BFF is not obligatory. In case of consideration by the Committee of a question connected with a club's execution of its obligations raised by the present point, the club and/or the football player, associations under its requirements should present corresponding documents.

365. Coaches and administrative and medical personnel also conclude contracts with football clubs. Thus, the Regulations concerning relations between the club and its employees extend equally to football players, coaches and administrative and medical workers.

366. The contract concluded between a club and a football player can be stopped on the basis provided by BFF Regulations and/or the legislation of Belarus. Contracts with a football player who has lost their work capacity in connection with a labour mutilation (trauma) or occupational disease received at training, gatherings or games cannot be unilaterally terminated at the initiative of the football club. Thus, when the contract expires, the term of its action should be prolonged until the restoration of the football player's work capacity or the establishment of disability.

367. The contract cannot be terminated unilaterally by the football player or the club during a season. In case of a pre-scheduled cancellation of the contract by one of the parties, the club is obliged to notify its association within seven days along with the reasons for the pre-scheduled cancellation of the contract. Thus, in cases of pre-scheduled cancellation of the contract at the initiative of the club, in the absence of fault by the football player, the club must pay the player a monetary compensation defined by the sum of the monthly average income of a football player for this club; the cancellation of the contract is estimated from a date before the expiry of the term of its action.

368. On the expiry of the term of action of the contract concluded between the club and the football player, at its pre-scheduled cancellation date or at contract cancellation by the mutual consent of the parties, the football player has the right to conclude a new contract with any other club at their own discretion. Thus, their former club does not have the right to receive indemnification for preparation and training of this football player if the player has reached the age of 23. The football player, having the status of professional over three successive seasons and playing less than 10% of official matches in the current season in all competitions in which the club took part, can terminate the contract for this reason ahead of schedule, having submitted the corresponding statement to the relevant association fifteen days after the last official match for the club in the season.

369. The transfer of an operating contract of a football player to a new club is possible only in the event that all three parties (the player, the present club and the future club) involved in the situation agree. Thus, a football player has the right, in the last six months of their current contract, to conclude a contract with a new club interested in their services; the new club should inform the present club of the football player's intentions.

370. In the case of an exclusion of a club from participating in a competition or as members of the BFF, football players with an operating contract with this club receive the status of free agent. Thus, such a club loses the right to receive indemnification for the preparation and training of the football player. In this situation, the specified club is obliged to extinguish any debts against the football player completely.

371. Agents and other persons operating according to FIFA, UEFA and BFF rules can represent the interests of football players in their relations with football clubs if they possess a corresponding licence with FIFA. At the conclusion of a transfer, if a football player used the services of an agent to develop the contract in such a transfer, the contract of the football player with the club must reference this fact. In specified contracts, the nameplate data, licence number, licence period of validity, football association and first name, middle initial and last name of the agent should be accurately specified. If a football player does not use an agent, this fact also should be reflected in the contract.

IV. Transfer Contracts

372. On transferring a football player from one club to another, the contract must include the transfer conditions of the football player. Transfer of contracts can occur in the following cases:

(1) If, during the contract validity period, all parties (the football player, the current club and the future club) have agreed to the transfer of the football player.
(2) If, on the transfer of a football school pupil, a football player for an amateur football club is transferred to a professional football club.
(3) If the transfer of a football player from club to club is carried out under the terms of 'rent'.

373. At the conclusion of the contract transfer between clubs, the sum of indemnification for the preparation and training of the football player and other conditions of transfer must be included. Transfer of the contract, appendices, changes and additions is concluded in writing, signed page by page by the CEOs of the clubs, certified with the seals of both clubs and subject to obligatory registration with the association in triplicate. Transfer of the contract cannot occur between clubs by granting to the other party goods, works and services.

374. The basis for refusing to register the transfer of a contract and the changes and additions to it is non-observance by the parties of the transfer requirements established by the present Regulations, the current legislation of Belarus and the authorized documents and regulations of FIFA, UEFA and the BFF.

375. The club that has offered work to a football player to conclude a transfer of a contract and/or conclude a new contract with a football player should complete the following necessary actions: study the documents necessary for concluding the transfer of the contract and/or concluding a new contract with the football player, stipulate the player's working conditions and hold testing and/or medical inspection of the football player. Otherwise, the club will be obliged to pay the full sum of indemnification for the preparation and training of the football player.

376. The professional football player can be 'rented' to another club on the basis of a written agreement (the transfer contract) between the player and the given clubs. Such a contract should be signed by the heads of the clubs and assured by the seals of the clubs and the football player. The football player should sign a contract on the period of validity of the 'rent' transfer with the new club.

377. Transfer of a football player from one club to another club on the terms of 'rent' is considered as one transfer. Thus, the return of the football player to the former club from which they were transferred on the terms of 'rent' is not a transfer.

378. The minimum term of 'rent' of a football player should coincide with a time interval between two registration periods.

379. The club that has taken the player in 'rent' has no right to transfer the player to a third club without the written permission of the club that has transferred the player in 'rent' and the player.

380. A club wishing to conclude a contract with a football player who has not reached 23 years of age, but whose contract has either expired or terminated ahead of schedule in the order established by the Regulations, is not obliged to inform the former club of the football player. However, as soon as a new club signs a contract with a football player, it should, within seven days, direct an inquiry to the former club of the player about the sum of indemnification for the preparation and training of this football player. The former club of the football player, if it has the right to receive indemnification for preparation and training, is obliged within seven days from the date of the reference of other club to present, with observance of Article 22 of the Regulations, a document confirming the sum subject to payment. In case of the absence of objections and disputes for the sum of indemnification for preparation and training, the new club should pay the specified sum in the next sixteen days.

381. If both clubs cannot settle a dispute on the size of the indemnification sum to be paid for the preparation and training of the football player, the Committee considers it. The Committee has the right to request, and clubs are obliged to provide, the necessary documents proving the calculation of indemnification for preparation and training and/or other documents.

382. The compensatory sum should be provided to the club accepting the football player within thirty days from the date of the Committee decision. If, after that term, the former club advises their association that the sum has not been paid or has not been paid in full, the BFF has the right to apply penal sanctions against the guilty club.

383. A club, wishing to take advantage of the services of a player who has, at present, an operating contract with another club, is obliged to inform this club of their interest in this football player in writing prior to beginning negotiations with the player.

384. If the club interested in the transfer of the player does not receive an answer within fifteen days after inquiry, it is considered as a refusal from the club with which the player is connected at this time by contract. In this case, if the interested club enters into negotiations with the football player, bypassing the player's contracted club, or issues the player a contract or has the player take part in training or matches, the BFF has the right to apply disciplinary sanctions against the interested club according to the BFF Disciplinary Code.

V. Protection of Minors

385. According to FIFA Regulations on the status and transfers of football players, the international transfer of players can occur only when the player is 18 years of age or older. However, the given rule does not apply in the following cases:

(1) The player's parents move to a country in which the new club is located for reasons not linked to football.
(2) The transfer takes place within the territory of the European Union (EU) or European Economic Area (EEA) and the player is aged between 16 and 18. In this case, the new club must fulfil the following minimum obligations:
    (a) It shall provide the player with an adequate football education and/or training in line with the highest national standards.
    (b) It shall guarantee the player an academic and/or school and/or vocational education and/or training, in addition to their football education and/or training, which will allow the player to pursue a career other than football should they cease playing professional football.
    (c) It shall make all necessary arrangements to ensure that the player is looked after in the best possible way (optimum living standards with a host family or in club accommodation, appointment of a mentor at the club).
    (d) It shall, on registration of such a player, provide the relevant association with proof that it is complying with the aforementioned obligations.
(3) The player lives no further than 50 kilometres from a national border and the club with which the player wishes to be registered in the neighbouring association is also within 50 kilometres of that border. The maximum distance between the player's domicile and the club's headquarters shall be 100 kilometres. In such cases, the player must continue to live at home and the two associations concerned must give their explicit consent.

VI. Compensation Between Clubs

386. The order for the transfer of football players to or from clubs of foreign football associations (international transfers) is under the jurisdiction of the BFF; equally, the order for the definition and payment of indemnification for the preparation and training of football players at such transfers is established by FIFA Regulations, under the status and transfer of football players and other FIFA regulation documents.

387. At the transfer of a football player over 23 years of age, after the expiry of the term of action of their contract, indemnification for the preparation and training of the football player is not required.

388. Football players called on urgent military service temporarily pause the actions of their contracts with clubs. For football players who finish military service or service in law-enforcement bodies, but continue their performance as part of these services, indemnification is paid to the football team (club) the football player was contracted to when called to engage in military or law-enforcement service.

389. In the case when a football player, at the end of their urgent military service and contract expiration, does not express the desire to return to their original team and concludes a contract with another club, the duty for indemnification payment is assigned to this club.

390. In the case when a football player's contract has not expired during urgent military services, the football player is obliged to return to their former club.

391. A contract concluded with a football player engaged in military service is considered void.

392. Indemnification for the preparation and training of a football player is paid in the following cases:

(1) When the football player is awarded the status of a professional for the first time (concludes their first professional contract).
(2) At each transfer of the football player before reaching 23 years of age, depending on their status, including the transfer of the player from a football school or an amateur football club to a professional football club or the transfer of the player from one professional football club to another.

393. Indemnification for the preparation and training of a football player is not paid:

(1) If the former club terminates the contract with the football player without a good reason or the football player is allocated by the Committee the status of free agent as a consequence of a default of the contract obligations of the former club to this football player.
(2) At the transfer of the football player from one amateur football club to another amateur football club.
(3) At the transfer of the football player from a professional football club to an amateur football club, if the football player receives the status of amateur only if the football player does not restore their status as a professional within thirty months).
(4) At the transfer of a football player over the age of 23 after the expiry of the term of action of their contract.

394. If in a contract action, all parties (the football player, the former club and the new club) have agreed to the transfer of the player, the size of indemnification is coordinated on a contractual basis between the specified clubs; this concludes the transfer contract, according to an order established by the Regulations.

395. To settle the accounts between clubs when transferring football players between the ages of 14 and 23, and upon the expiry of a previous contract, the following requirements for determining the amount of compensation are set.

396. The sum of indemnification for preparation and training corresponds to the income of the football player in the club under their contract, for no more than the last five years. When increased by the factor categories of the club, this represents the maximum sum of indemnification for preparation and training. Income includes wages, all kinds of awards and extra charges. Monetary compensation paid by a football club to the football player on the pre-scheduled cancellation of a contract and the debts of a football club to a football player under the contract are not included as income.

397. Calculation of the income of the professional football player is defined in the following ways:

(1) The monthly income of the player in Belarusian roubles is translated to US dollars by its division into the sum corresponding to an official rate of the National Bank of Belarus on the first date of each subsequent month.
(2) The revenue of the player is defined by USD through an exchange rate established by the National Bank of Belarus at the moment of transferring the money.
(3) The following categories of clubs and order of application of category factors are established:
   (a) first category – football clubs of the higher league;
   (b) second category – football clubs of the first league;
   (c) third category – football clubs of the second league;
   (d) fourth category – amateur soccer teams participating in regional competitions.

398. Club categories are defined following the results of the completed championship.

399. At the transfer of a football player from a club of the first category to another club of the first category, a factor of three is applied; at the transfer of a football player from a club of the first category to a club of the second category, a factor of two is applied; at the transfer of a football player from a club of the first category to a club of the third category, a factor of one is applied.

400. At the transfer of a football player from a club of the second category to a club of the first category, a factor of three is applied; at the transfer of the football player from a club of the second category to another club of the second category, a factor of two is applied; at the transfer of a football player from a club of the second category to a club of the third category, a factor of one is applied.

401. At the transfer of a football player from a club of the third category to a club of the first category, a factor of three is applied; at the transfer of a football player from a club of the third category to a club of the second category, a factor of two is applied; at the transfer of a football player from a club of the third category to another club of the third category, a factor of one is applied.

402. At the transfer of a football player from clubs of the first, second and third categories to a club of the fourth category, indemnification for preparation and training is not paid. At the transfer of a football player from a club of the fourth category to a club of the first category, a factor of three is applied; at the transfer of a football player from a club of the fourth category to a club of the second category, a factor of two is applied; at the transfer of a football player from a club of the fourth category to a club of the third category, a factor of one is applied; at the transfer of a football player from a club of the fourth category to another club of the fourth category, indemnification for preparation and training is not paid.

403. Football players of more than 23 years of age, whose contract terms have expired, may be transferred to other football clubs without payment of indemnification for preparation and training.

404. The size of indemnification for preparation and training at the transfer of a football player from a club of the fourth category to clubs of the first and second categories corresponds to 100 baseline values,[79] increased by the factor category of the club.

405. According to Article 19(1) of the present Regulations, the compensatory sum for preparation and training of the football player is subject to payment by the new club no later than thirty days after signing the contract with the football player if the clubs involved do not agree otherwise about other. In cases of target date infringement, the BFF can subject the guilty club to disciplinary sanctions according to the BFF Disciplinary Code.

406. If the football player, having an operating contract, is at another club on the terms of 'rent', calculation of indemnification for the preparation and training is made using the income of the football player during their work before the transfer to the other club on the terms of 'rent' and/or after the termination of the terms of 'rent', but not for more than five years.

407. A football club and a football player can enter into an agreement in writing, or include in the contract, a situation in which the football club refuses the right to indemnification for preparation and training after the expiry of the contract validity period and the transfer of the football player to another club.

79. Baseline value on 1 Aug. 2020 is BYN 27 (about USD 11.02).

408. If the club with the right to receive indemnification for the preparation and training of the football player according to the Regulations does not declare this right within two years after the football player has signed their first contract as a professional or has transferred to another professional club, indemnification for the preparation and training of this football player is paid in favour of the association.

VII. Transfer of Minors, Studies in Sporting Schools, Compensation for Minors

409. A young football player, between the ages of 8 and 18, wishing to transfer from one football school (club) to another, preserving their status as an amateur player, should observe the following procedure:

(1) The young football player and their parents should address a written statement to the head of a football school in which they are engaged about their desire to transfer to another football school. In the statement, the motives for the transfer should be stated. The head of the football school the young football player plans to transfer to should inform in writing the football school the young football player currently attends about their consent (or disagreement) to accept him. In case of an absence of contradictions between the organizations, the football school in which the young football player was engaged provides written permission, transfers the passport of the football player and includes the changes on the passport of the football player, according to the rules established in Article 6(2) of the Regulations.
(2) If the parties have not come to an agreement, the football school the young football player wishes to transfer to addresses the regional federation for permission to resolve the dispute. The regional federation should consider the situation and make a decision within fifteen days. The decision of the regional federation can be appealed to the Committee.

410. A young football player between the ages of 12 and 14 can transfer to another football school with a corresponding registration of the transfer only in the case of the parents of the young football player moving to a constant residence in other areas of the city of Minsk or another city of Belarus or in other significant circumstances. All transfers between these ages are considered by the regional federations of football with observance of the BFF Regulations.

411. Clubs wishing to conclude a contract with young football players over the age of 14, for whom it will be their first professional contract, should observe the following procedure.

412. A club applying for a young football player between the ages of 14 and 18 are obliged, prior to beginning negotiations with the young football player and their lawful representatives, to address in writing to the head of the football school in which the given football player is engaged their desire to conclude a contract with the young football player (the club directs copies of the reference to the regional federation and the BFF). The head of the football school is obliged to inform their regional federation and association of the intent. The associations and regional federations keep account of the offers for each young football player at each football school.

413. In cases when several clubs are interested in one young football player, the association organizes a 'football call', depending on the terms of the applications. The club that offers the best conditions to the football school and the young football player gets the rights to the football player; therefore, the club should conclude a transfer contract with the football school and a professional contract with the football player. In the text of the transfer contract, the size of indemnification for preparation and training shall be determined on the transfer of the young football player; terms are specified as a mutual settlement of accounts between the parties. After signing the transfer contract, the football school in which the young football player was engaged provides written permission, transfers the passport of the football player to the club and records the changes in the passport of the football player according to the rules established in Article 6(2) of the Regulations.

414. With a view of ordering the transfers of young football players, transfers are carried out two times during the registration periods established by the BFF.

415. When a football player turns 18 and neither the player nor their football school (club) has received offers of transfer, that football player is considered belonging to the given football school (club) for the next thirty months.

416. Transfer rights to a football player attending a sporting school for the purpose of performance for a national team of Belarus, for the period of training at the sporting school and after it, remain with the football school (club) delegating the football player to the sporting school. Thus, the BFF, under the offer of a sporting school, should send a letter of inquiry to the head of the football school (club). Representatives of a sporting school have no right to enter into negotiations with the football player without notifying the head of the football school (club).

417. The professional football player selected by the BFF and enlisted in a sporting school for the purpose of playing for a national team of Belarus should return to the football club they were previously engaged with after the termination of training (the pre-scheduled termination of training); throughout the next two years, the player should continue to support this football club and the club and the player should sign a new contract for the above-stated term. Refusal of any of the parties to sign the new contract will attract the application of sanctions against the guilty party, provided for by the present Regulations for wrongful cancellation of an operating contract, with an additional penal sanction at a rate of 500 base sizes.[80]

80. About EUR 10.50 in February 2019.

418. After the termination of training (the pre-scheduled termination of training) in a sporting school, the player is obliged to inform the football school (club) delegating the football player of this event.

419. During the training of a young football player in a sporting school, the last club receives indemnification for the preparation and training of the football player, proportional to the volume of time spent by the player in these establishments.

420. At the transfer of a young football player from one football school (club) to another, with preservation of their amateur status, indemnification for their preparation and training is not paid.

421. Transfer of a football player from a football school to a club occurs via contract, in which the club undertakes to pay indemnification for the preparation and training of the football player to all football schools, including sporting schools, that took part in the preparation and training of the football player while they were between the ages of 12 and 23, according to the passport of the football player. Indemnification for preparation and training should be paid within six months from the moment of contract signing between the club and the young football player.

422. The size and order of payment of compensation for the training and education of young players are established by the Council of Ministers of the Republic of Belarus. Clubs are responsible for the correctness of the calculation of the payment amount and the timeliness of its payment.

423. Compensation for training and education of young players does not include:

(1) the transition of a young football player, with the conservation of amateur status, from one school football (club) to another;
(2) the first employment or civil contract the football player concludes with the organizations carrying out their athletic training;
(3) the sports training carried out at the player's own expense (or at the expense of the player's legal representatives).

424. The coach who trained the young football player who has concluded their first professional contract with a club should receive not less than 20% (after a deduction of all obligatory payments according to the legislation of Belarus) of the sum specified in the contract between the club and football school (club).

425. If there are several coaches who have participated in the training of a football player, the paid sum is shared among them depending on the time spent in the player's preparation and training.

426. If a football club and/or football school enter into negotiations for a transfer with a football player, bypassing their club (school), or has the player take part in training, matches or travel abroad or issues the football player a contract, the BFF has the right to apply to such football club (school) disciplinary sanctions according to the BFF Disciplinary Code.

VIII. Contract Stability

427. For a football player who signed a contract before the age of 28 and has terminated it without a valid excuse or without a sufficient basis from a sporting point of view within the first three years of action of the contract (in the so-called protected period), the association can implement corresponding sanctions, according to FIFA Regulations, under the status and transfers of football players. A contract signed after the age of 28 includes the same principles, but only within the first two years.

428. For a football player who has signed a contract before turning 28 years of age and terminated it without a valid excuse or without sufficient basis from a sporting point of view after the first three years of action of the contract, and for a football player who has signed a contract at the age of 28 years and terminated it without valid excuse or without sufficient basis from a sporting point of view after the first two years of action of the contract, the sanctions are not applied, if, within fifteen days after carrying out the last official match of a club in a current season, the player directs the notice for contract cancellation to the association.

429. In case of cancellation of the contract without a good reason, the guilty party should pay monetary compensation. If contract cancellation occurs unilaterally at the initiative of the football player without sufficient basis or during the protected period, the football player should pay monetary compensation to the former club at a rate of the received income in this club, but for no more than three years.

430. The right to payment and receipt of monetary compensation cannot be transferred to a third party. Thus, if the football player pays monetary compensation, subsidiary responsibility for payment of this compensation is borne by the new club.

431. For a football player recognized as being guilty of infringing the contract during the protected period, in addition to a duty to pay monetary compensation, the following disciplinary sanctions can be inflicted:

(1) disqualification for four months;
(2) in the presence of aggravating circumstances, disqualification for six months.

432. In all cases, such disciplinary sanctions should come into force from the beginning of the following season with a new club.

433. Contract cancellation unilaterally without a good reason or without a good sporting reason, after the expiry of the term of the protected period, should not attract any disciplinary sanctions. However, sanctions can be imposed if the football player has not properly notified the association and the former club of the contract cancellation (i.e., within fifteen days after the last official match of a season). The protected period renews at the prolongation of the previous contract.

434. In addition to subsidiary responsibility for payment of monetary compensation for the club convicted of infringing a contract or prompting a football player to break a contract during the protected period, disciplinary sanctions should be inflicted. It is supposed, if not proved otherwise, that any club that has signed a contract with a football player who has broken off a contract without a good reason had compelled the player to make the infringement. This club is forbidden to register new players for two registration periods.

435. According to FIFA Regulations and other documents, under the status and transfers of football players, FIFA, UEFA and BFF disciplinary sanctions also are imposed on any other persons (football players, officials of club, agents of football players), operating for the purpose of prompting a player to break their operating contract.

IX. National Team Players

436. Directing of players to appropriate selected teams is binding upon receipt of the corresponding call for participation in training activities in preparation for competitions.

437. Competitions and international matches are stipulated in the FIFA international match calendar (the international window) for the final competitions of national teams held by FIFA, UEFA, as well as other competitions held by FIFA, UEFA, the BFF or any special decisions of these organizations.

438. The international window is defined as a nine-day period, beginning Monday morning and ending the next Tuesday night, which is reserved for teams in the international competition. During the international window, a maximum of two matches for each national team can be held, regardless of whether these official matches are qualified as FIFA competitions, UEFA competitions or championships.

439. These matches can be scheduled on any day during the international window, provided that at least two full calendar days remain between two matches (e.g., Thursday-Sunday or Saturday-Tuesday).

440. Each national team has the right to hold two matches in the international window on the territory of a confederation, with one exception – playoffs for FIFA official competitions between teams of different confederations.

441. If at least some of the matches are friendly matches, the matches may be held in two different confederations only if the distance between the places of matches is less than five hours of flight under the official scheduled airlines and the two time zones.

442. For the international window, players have to be released to join the national team no later than Monday morning and should return to their club no later than the next Wednesday morning after the completion of the international window.

443. For the final competition conducted by FIFA, UEFA players must be released to their teams no later than the Monday morning of the week preceding the week when starting respective final competitions and shall be exempt by association on the morning after the last match of their teams in the tournament.

444. Footballers called by their national associations on the conditions of this chapter shall return to their responsibilities with their clubs not later than twenty-four hours after completion of the corresponding exemption period for which they were summoned. This period must be extended to forty-eight hours when matches were held in a different confederation to the one in which the player is a club member. Clubs should be informed in writing of the player's route of travel forth and back ten days before the beginning of the release period for the player. The association shall ensure the return of a player to their club after a match.

445. The national association calling upon the football player refunds the player for journey expenses and any expenses actually suffered by the football player as a result of such a call.

446. The club in which the called football player is registered bears responsibility for the player's insurance, covering illness and/or accident for all periods of exemption, including insurance for injuries sustained during the international match for which the player has been released.

447. The contract between the club and the football player who is called into a national team cannot be suspended or terminated by a club unilaterally.

448. Any football player, having the right to participate in the national teams of Belarus according to FIFA rules and called for one of the Belarus national teams, is obliged to answer a call from the BFF to participate in the structure of a corresponding national team of Belarus in training and/or matches. If such a football player cannot obey the call from BFF because of a trauma or illness, they should agree on medical inspection by a doctor recommended by the BFF.

449. The BFF, intending to have a football player play abroad, is obliged to notify the player and their club in writing not less than fifteen days prior to the date of the match in which the participation of this football player is necessary. The club is obliged to confirm the clearing of the football player within six days from the date of receipt of the notice by the club.

450. The BFF has the right to address to FIFA a request for help in granting clearance to a football player playing abroad only in the following two circumstances:

(1) The request to interfere has been directed to the national association in which the football player is registered; however, this request has not been satisfied.
(2) This business should be directed to FIFA at least five days prior to the date of the match in which the participation of the given football player is required.

451. A football player called by the BFF to join one of the national teams of Belarus does not have, under any circumstances, the right to support the club in which they are registered during the period in which they have been released or should be released. Moreover, such restrictions for the club lasts for five days if the football player, for any reason, did not want or was unable to obey a call.

452. If the club refuses to release the player or neglects the duties outlined in the Regulations, the ABFF should declare a defeat to the club in the relevant match with the participation of the unreleased football player and victory to the contending club in the specified match. In the event that matches played acceding to the elimination system, the guilty club appears lost, irrespective of the result of the first (repeated) match.

X. Jurisdiction of Status and Transfer Matters

453. According to the Charter, the association possesses the higher jurisdiction on questions addressed to it concerning members of the ABFF, sportspeople, coaches, proprietors of football clubs and other employees related to contracts or other legalized relations with football clubs.

454. The competence of the ABFF includes consideration of the following:

(1) Conflicts between clubs, players and coaches concerning maintenance of contract stability, relations for hiring and disciplinary actions and/or indemnifications for contract infringement.
(2) Conflicts on an international scale concerning hiring between clubs and players and/or the collective agreement while at a national level are resolved by an association, the independent arbitration court guaranteeing a fair legal investigation and observing a principle of equality of players and clubs may be created.
(3) Conflicts concerning payment of indemnification for preparation and the mechanism of FIFA solidarity between clubs.
(4) Other conflicts according to the standard documents of FIFA and the BFF.

455. When considering the above-stated question, the BFF, according to the Charter, founded two proxy bodies. The first is the Committee on the Status and Transfer of Football Players and the second is Football Arbitration. Descriptions of procedures and Committee activities are provided in the Regulations on Committees established by the Executive Committee; the procedural issues and activities of Football Arbitration are provided in the Regulations on the activity of Football Arbitration established by the Conference.

§2. Ice Hockey

456. In 2011, the Federation of Ice Hockey of Republic of Belarus (FHRB) approved the rules 'On the Status of the Hockey Player' (updated version: 11 July 2018), regulating the legal status, rights and duties of hockey players, the procedure for registration and the rules for admitting hockey players to participate in competitions operated by the FHRB, the order for registering contract relations between hockey players and hockey clubs, the rules for the transfer of hockey players and the size and order of compensatory payments for the preparation of hockey players.

I. The Legal Status, Rights and Duties of Hockey Players

457. A hockey player may have the following statuses:

(1) Under current contract
(2) A restricted free agent
(3) An unrestricted free agent
(4) A junior
(5) Under conflict
(6) Fixed rights.

When determining the status of a hockey player, the age of the player is determined by the age of the player at the beginning of the season and is valid throughout the season.

458. The professional hockey player has the right to:

(1) Engage in labour as the worthiest way to assert oneself, as well as healthy and safe working conditions.
(2) Protected economic and social rights and interests.
(3) Participate in meetings.
(4) Timely and full payment of wages and salaries and other types of remuneration in accordance with their qualifications, the complexity of the work, the quantity and quality of work performed and other payments due to the hockey player in the amount and on the terms as provided for in the fixed-term employment contract.
(5) Daily and weekly rest and vacations, the duration of the period not less than that established by the LC.
(6) Social insurance, pensions and guarantees in the event of occupational disease, work-related injury, disability and loss of employment.

(7) Obtain sports categories and sports titles meeting the standards and requirements of the sports classification.
(8) Promote the protection of the rights and legitimate interests of hockey players in international sports organizations.
(9) Appeal to the FHRB Appeals Committee in relation to hockey player status.
(10) Receive from the club, in case of early termination of the labour contract, salary (remuneration) for the actual time worked and other payments in accordance with the law.
(11) Outside employment with another employer as an athlete, only with the permission of the club, which is the employer of the main place of work.
(12) Non-interference in privacy and respect for privacy.
(13) Judicial and other protection of labour rights.
(14) Other rights established by labour legislation.

459. The professional hockey player is obliged to:

(1) Comply with internal work regulations, the status of the hockey player and other documents regulating labour discipline issues.
(2) Perform the written and oral orders and instructions of the club, not contrary to legislation and local regulations of the club.
(3) Take part in sports competitions only on the club's instructions.
(4) Avoid actions that interfere with other workers performing their duties.
(5) Comply with the regulatory legal acts of the Republic of Belarus, local acts and the occupational safety requirements of the club on using personal protective equipment.
(6) Treat the club's property with care, use it for the performance of work provided for by the employment contract and take measures to prevent damage.
(7) Observe the established procedure for keeping documents of material and monetary value.
(8) Provide exclusive gaming services and knowledge, skills and abilities only to the club, to work out the established labour contract and not to enter into any employment contracts and not to negotiate employment contracts with other hockey clubs and organizations of the Republic of Belarus and abroad for the entire period of operation of this fixed-term employment contract;
(9) Not to act for any other team and not to take part in other sporting events, including national teams of the Republic of Belarus, without the written permission of the club's management.
(10) Strictly observe the club's Charter, the association's Charter, the Ice Hockey Federation of the Republic of Belarus (FHROB) and the provisions for the status of the hockey player, as well as the requirements of the fixed-term employment contract, the Federal Hockey Federation and the International Ice Hockey Federation (IIHF), including the rules on transfers to other clubs.
(11) Comply with all requirements of club management and coaching compositions related to professional education, training and play practice; work with full dedication to complete timely and qualitatively approved work plans and standards.

(12) Participate in national and international travel using unconditional routes and vehicles offered by the club.
(13) Always be in optimal sports condition throughout the hockey season and be ready to play in all matches held by the club.
(14) Maintain a high level of fitness for the performance of their obligations under this fixed-term employment contract – a professional hockey player is obliged to comply with the sports regime, to carry out the preparation plans for competition and to appear at training classes at the day and time appointed by management.
(15) Attend all medical examinations and engage in the restoration activities organized by the Club.
(16) Act outside the hockey pitch in accordance with high standards of honesty, morality, fair play and sportsmanship and not harm the club and professional hockey in general with their behaviour.
(17) Continue regular training if temporarily unable to play games or if exposed to temporary disqualification.
(18) Not take drugs, anabolic drugs and potent or stimulating drugs that can lead to the disqualification of the professional hockey player and the deterioration of their health; take necessary medicines as agreed with the club's doctor.
(19) Not to receive money, bonuses or valuable gifts from individuals or organizations for achieving victory in unsportsmanlike matches or attempt to otherwise influence the outcome of any particular meeting or series of games; report such facts immediately to the head coach or club management.
(20) Transfer to the club for the period of the employment contract all rights to use their image and name for advertising and marketing purposes without charging any additional fees.
(21) Not disclose to third parties, without the club's consent, during the whole period of validity of the fixed-term employment contract and five years after its expiration (dissolution), anything that became known to them during their work at the club. The following data is a trade secret:
   - special and legal documentation available at the club, including accounting and statistical information;
   - information related to the financial operations of the club itself and its business partners;
   - information related to the execution of their own obligations, including the amount of the established monetary remuneration;
   - information related to the activities of the club and its partners, including the commercial, legal and scientific developments that are the property of the club.
(22) Bear full material liability for damage caused to the club by the fault of the professional hockey player.
(23) Make every effort to perform the tasks assigned to the team, to continuously and steadily improve their sporting level, to work with full commitment and to comply with all legal orders of the team's management and the club. Otherwise, the club may revise bonus payments and, in exceptional cases determined by the present employment contract and legislation, terminate the fixed-term employment contract early unilaterally.

(24) Make a cash payment to the club upon termination of the fixed-term employment contract in the cases provided for in the fixed-term employment agreement and in the established data.
(25) Take part in sports competitions only on the orders of the coaching staff and management of the club.
(26) Observe the rules of hockey competitions with regards to the following: puck and regulations (rules of conduct) for events of the competitions they are taking part in.
(27) Take part in challenges (applications) to the republican public administration, to pursue public policy in the field of physical education and sport, or to FHRB for sporting events in the composition of the national teams of the Republic of Belarus in sports.
(28) Undergo doping control in accordance with the legislation on physical education and sport.
(29) Attend medical check-ups in the manner prescribed by law.
(30) Inform the head coach and the club's management immediately about their health status and notify them of any illness, including the number of injuries and other health problems.
(31) Maintain the reputation of the employer during public media appearances.
(32) Not participate in betting and/or betting games, as well as other gambling games in which winning directly or indirectly depends on the results of sports competitions the player or the player's club team participates in.

II. Registration of Hockey Players with FHRB

460. The relationship between the club and the hockey player is based on an employment contract. This agreement is subject to mandatory registration by the Federation in accordance with the established procedure. It is necessary to note that the hockey player has no right to take part in the championship without the presence of the employment contract (or for students, a Sports Training Agreement), registered in the Federation.

461. The employment contract between the club and the hockey player can have the following varieties:

(1) a first employment contract;
(2) a review contract;
(3) a Sports Training Agreement.

III. First Employment Contract

462. The first employment contract of a hockey player should be understood as the employment contract concluded between students of sports schools who have junior status, graduates of sports schools and clubs, the subject of which is the implementation of activities in the field of professional sports.

463. The first employment contract may be signed with students who have attained junior status and who have reached the age of 16; the term of validity of such an employment contract shall expire on 30 April of the year the hockey player turns 20.

464. The club has a preferential right to conclude the first employment contract with the students of sports schools, having the status of junior, provided that sports school is part of the club structure or there is an agreement of cooperation between the club and sports school and, where available, agreement on the registered qualification offer to such student (at the conclusion of the first employment contract after graduating from training at the sports school).

465. Upon termination of the first employment contract, the club has the right to make a new qualification offer to a hockey player in accordance with the requirements provided for in Article 3 of this Statute.

466. In the event that the club uses its priority right to conclude the first employment contract with a student of sports school with junior status, subject to the conditions provided for in Article 15, paragraph 3, of the present Statute, a student of a sports school who has junior status or a sports school graduate must conclude with the club their first employment contract.

467. If the club has not offered to a student of a sports school with junior status a qualification offer before the 5 May graduation from the sports school, or the student, by 30 April of the year of graduation from sports school, did not enter into a first employment contract and the term of validity of the sports training agreement with the sports school has expired, the player is given the status of unrestricted free agent.

IV. Rules for the Transfer of Hockey Players and an Order for Compensatory Payments

468. A hockey player who has a valid employment contract can be transferred (exchanged) to another club, as well as to a club of the FHRB, from the moment of concluding the first employment contract.

469. A hockey player aged 27 years or older may, upon signing an employment contract, refuse to be transferred (exchanged) to a specific club or transferred (exchanged) in general, which must be recorded in the employment contract.

470. The transfer of a hockey player(s) to another club may be made in the following ways:

(1) Transfer of a hockey player to another club for a certain period of time with the conclusion of a cooperation agreement between the clubs for monetary compensation or no compensation;

(2) Transfer of sports rights to another club with or without monetary compensation;
(3) Counter-exchange of hockey players, in which case it is allowed to exchange an unequal number of hockey players;
(4) Counter payment of monetary compensation to the club (amount of compensation is determined by agreement of the parties (clubs);
(5) By reciprocal provision to the club (exchange) of sports rights in respect of the hockey player(s) with the status of conflict or fixed rights;
(6) By counter-providing any combination of conditions, provided for in subparagraphs (1) to (5) of this paragraph (mixed transfer agreement).

471. Before entering into a transfer agreement (exchange) or a cooperation agreement, the clubs are obliged to familiarize themselves with all terms and conditions of the current employment contracts of the hockey players. After signing the transfer agreement (exchange) of the claim under the terms and conditions, the hockey players of the Federal Hockey Fund are not eligible for employment contracts.

472. In case of agreement on all terms of transfer or hockey player(s) exchange, clubs are required to sign a transfer agreement (exchange) for the hockey player(s) in the prescribed form (Annex 8) or a cooperation agreement (Annex 5). Hockey player(s) should be acquainted with these contracts and should sign them.

473. Transfer (exchange) may be made no later than the closing date of the transfer window for the current sports season (until 24:00, Belarusian time).

474. In the case of a transfer of a hockey player to another role within a club in the Championship of the Republic of Belarus, the new club and the hockey player are generally obliged to conclude an employment contract under the same conditions as those set out in the player's employment contract with the previous club. The terms of remuneration are not allowed to change in the direction of improvement. The terms of remuneration are allowed to change in the direction of deterioration, provided that the hockey player agrees to such deterioration. Additional consent of the hockey player to transfer to another role under a transfer agreement (exchange) or cooperation agreement is not required. A new employment contract is subject to mandatory registration with the FHRB.

475. The employment contract of a hockey player with the previous club, and the hockey players themselves, are subject to dismissal by transfer to another employer in accordance with applicable law.

476. The club must notify the hockey player in writing of transfer (exchange) by personal delivery of the notice or by sending it by registered letter with a notice of delivery. The notice must contain information about the transfer (exchange), the name and location of the new club and the time and place of arrival at the new club.

477. All costs for moving a hockey player (including transportation costs) shall be borne by the club hosting the player.

478. A transfer agreement (exchange) or cooperation agreement must be sent to the FHRB within twenty-four hours of its signing (by fax or email). The original contract must be sent to the FHRB for registration within five days after the signing by the clubs.

V. Rules for the Transfer of Professional Hockey Players

479. A professional hockey player has the right to transfer from one hockey club to another hockey club in the following cases:

(1) after the expiry of the contract between the professional hockey player and a hockey club;
(2) on achievement of a joint arrangement between two hockey clubs and the hockey player about the player's transfer before the termination of the period of validity of the player's contract;
(3) on registration of the pre-scheduled cancellation of the contract, under the mutual arrangement of the hockey player and the hockey club.

480. The basis for the transfer of a hockey player with the status of restricted free agent to a new club is the transfer agreement concluded between the clubs. The transfer agreement provided for in this article is concluded in three copies and must be registered with the FHRB within twenty-four hours after signing. The original contract must be sent to the FHRB within five days after its signing by the clubs.

481. In the case of the transfer of a hockey player (signing of an employment contract) with the status of restricted free agent, the old club is owed compensation, which is calculated on the basis of the weighted average remuneration for qualification and contract proposals.

482. The hockey player to whom the club has made the qualification offer provided for in Article 3 of this Statute acquires the status of restricted free agent effective 6 May.

483. A hockey player with the status of restricted free agent has the right to accept the contract offer of a hockey club registered for the Championship of Belarus or the Continental Hockey League, from 6 May to 15 May (until 24:00, Belarusian time).

484. The qualification proposal must contain:

(1) the name of the hockey club;
(2) the name, surname, patronymic and date of birth of the hockey player;
(3) the term of validity for the proposed employment agreement;

(4) the amount of the contracted sum for the month and for the season, excluding compensation, incentives and social payments.

A qualification proposal can be made to the hockey player starting from the first day following the day of the last game of the current sports season until 5 May of the season following the current, inclusive (until 24:00, Belarusian time).

485. A qualification proposal can be made:

> To a hockey player, starting from the first day following the day of the last game of the current sports season until 5 May of the season following the current one, inclusive (till 24:00, Belarusian time). On 6 May of the corresponding calendar year, the FHRB publishes the list of qualification proposals on the official website of the FHRB.

486. If the hockey club that made a qualifying offer (the previous club) until 20 May (until 24:00, Belarusian time) repeats the terms of the contract proposal (term and contract amount) and the hockey player goes to the new club (except for Belarusian hockey clubs performing in the Continental Hockey League) from which the player accepted the contract proposal, payment of compensation by this club to the previous club is mandatory. The amount of compensation is determined from the calculations provided for in Article 27 of the present Statute.

487. If the hockey player does not enter into an employment contract with the new club before the official due date of the preseason fees, the new club has the right to withdraw the contract offer. The rights to the hockey player remain with the previous club. If a hockey player is unable to conclude an employment contract due to the refusal of the new club, the hockey player is obliged to inform the FHRB in writing about the situation by 1 July of the current sports season.

488. If a hockey player, who has received a qualifying bid and has not submitted a contract proposal to another club or has received a repetition of terms of the contract proposal from their previous club, refuses to enter into an employment agreement before the date of the official start of the preseason training camp of the current sports season, the hockey player shall be assigned the status of fixed rights (Article 9(1) of the current Statute). From the closing date of the transfer window of the current sports season, the player loses the right to take part in games in the current sports season. All sports rights to the hockey player are assigned to the previous club.

489. A hockey player acquires the status of an unlimited free agent in the following cases:

(1) if the hockey player has reached the age of 27 or older and the period of validity for their employment contract expired at the end of the sports season when they reached the age of 27 years and older;

(2) if the term of validity of the employment contract expired at the end of the current sports season and the hockey player has not received a qualifying offer in the manner prescribed by this Statute;
(3) if the employment agreement with the club is terminated by agreement of the parties or at the initiative of the club (except for termination on grounds relating to disciplinary sanctions, transfer to other work or exchange) and in the absence of a cooperation agreement between the clubs;
(4) in case of registration of the agreement by the FHRB on refusal to conclude the employment contract provided for in paragraph 10 of Article 5 of the present Statute.

490. The hockey player, having received the status of unrestricted free agent, has the right to conduct negotiations with any club. The player's former club loses the priority right to the conclusion of a new contract.

491. The hockey player has no right to training or employment in other clubs (hockey schools) before full legal registration of their transfer with the conclusion of the contract between their previous club and new club (hockey school).

VI. Time for the Transfer of Professional Hockey Players

492. The hockey player has the right to temporarily support other hockey clubs in the presence of a written arrangement between the hockey club with which the contract of the professional hockey player is concluded and the club that the hockey player is temporarily supporting.

493. In the case of a hockey player transferring to another role at a hockey club competing in the Championship of the Republic of Belarus, the new club and the hockey player generally conclude an employment contract under the same conditions that were fixed in the player's employment contract with the previous club. The terms of remuneration are not allowed to change in the direction of improvement but are allowed to change, subject to the consent of the hockey player, in the direction of deterioration. Obtaining additional consent from the hockey player to transfer to another role on a transfer agreement (exchange) or a cooperation agreement is not required. A new employment contract must be concluded and registered with the FHRB.

VII. Order of the Resolution of Disputes

494. The relationship between the club and the hockey player is subject to initial review by the Appeals Committee.

495. If a hockey player joins any other hockey club, including a foreign club, without the written permission of the club, then the hockey player and the club agree in the event of a dispute to the exclusive jurisdiction of the Appeals Committee of the FHRB and acknowledge that the decision of the Appeals Committee of the FHRB prohibiting the player from playing for any other hockey club, including foreign, have full force and effect in the Republic of Belarus and in any other country, and the hockey player agrees not to appeal against the decisions of the Appeals Committee of the FHRB prohibiting a hockey player from playing for any other hockey club, including a foreign club.

496. Decisions of the FHRB Appeals Committee are final and are not subject to appeal or review.

497. The club and the hockey player agree that the terms, conditions and services provided by the hockey player under the employment contract are unique, invaluable and the club cannot be adequately compensated. Therefore, in the case of reasonable claims, the club is entitled to demand and receive, through the appropriate authorities of the IIHF and the FHRB, judicial and disciplinary procedures for the prohibition of a hockey player to compete for any other hockey club, including a foreign club. These terms and conditions do not restrict in any way the rights of the club to make any other claims of the hockey player.

498. According to Article 48 of the LPCS, sports disputes are resolved in Belarus by courts, in accordance with the law, as well as with the use of alternative methods of dispute resolution permitted in accordance with the law, including through mediation and arbitration.

Part III. Doping and Sport

Chapter 1. General Issues

499. The Ministry of Sports and Tourism defines an order of the deprivation of the right to participate in the official sports competitions of Belarus, in international sports competitions and in the national teams of Belarus for sportspeople whose biotests have shown the use of forbidden methods and substances, persons guilty of encouraging sportspeople to engage in this use and sportspeople who have refused anti-doping control (Point 6.7 of Positions of the Ministry). This is conducted via the general management of the Belarus organization for anti-doping control in the field of sport (Point 5 of Positions of the Ministry).

500. Sports federations define anti-doping policies according to provisions of the national legislation and legal acts of their relevant IFs, such as the IOC and the World Anti-Doping Agency (WADA).

Chapter 2. Public Regulations

501. Doping control includes the stages and processes established by the Regulation on Anti-Doping Rules of the Republic of Belarus, taking into account WADA (Article 50(3) LPCS).

502. Doping control applies to all sportspeople, irrespective of their status, age, level of skill and residence by way of and on the conditions stipulated by the Regulation on Anti-Doping Rules of the Republic of Belarus (Article 50(4) LPCS).

503. Doping control of members of the national sports teams of Belarus, secondary school students at Olympic reserve schools and specialized sports classes in general secondary education institutions, students attending specialized training and sports facilities and child and youth sports schools (specialized child and youth schools for Olympic reserves) included in the structure of sports clubs as separate structural subdivisions participating in sporting events, conducted by the decision of the National Anti-Doping Agency (NADA), is paid from the means of the State budget (Article 50(5) LPCS).

504. The persons responsible for managing sports events are obliged to provide conditions for carrying out anti-doping control (Article 50(6) LPCS).

505. Sportspeople, coaches and other persons who are guilty of doping in sport are liable in accordance with the Regulation on Anti-Doping Rules of the Republic of Belarus, other legislative acts and the decisions of relevant international sports organizations (Article 49(6) LPCS).

506. Sports results obtained with the use of prohibited methods or substances can be made void by the persons responsible for managing competitions (Article 49(4) LPCS).

507. Pupils of sporting schools are obliged not to interfere with anti-doping control. A pupil can be removed from a specialized sports educational establishment for the use of methods or substances promoting the increase of working capacity and forbidden for use by the legislation of Belarus and (or) decisions of the IOC and other corresponding international organizations, or for being an obstacle to carrying out anti-doping control.

508. By the decision of the Council of Ministers of Belarus dated 19 January 2006, No. 61[81] (updated version: 17 August 2020), the Interdepartmental Coordination Anti-Doping Council within the Council of the Ministry of the Republic Belarus was created. The Interdepartmental Coordination Anti-Doping Council (hereinafter 'the Council') was created to perfect the interaction of state bodies,

81. The National Register of Legal Acts of Belarus, 2 Feb. 2006, No. 19, 5/17163.

physical training and sports organizations and other organizations in realizing the state policy directed at preventing the use of substances and methods forbidden in sports.

509. The Council is a coordinating body that operates on a constant basis. The Council is guided by the Constitution of Belarus, the LPCS, other legal acts of Belarus, the legal documents of WADA, the rules of international sports organizations and its own Rules.

510. The primary goals of the Council are to:

(1) Coordinate the interactions of state bodies, physical training, sports organizations and other anti-doping agencies.
(2) Control the efficiency of measures accepted in Belarus on the suppression of forbidden substances and methods in sport.
(3) Render assistance:
  (a) in the development and realization of republican programmes on disputes over anti-doping control;
  (b) in carrying out a uniform policy on preventive measures for the use of forbidden substances and methods;
  (c) in the study of a positive experience of foreign states and international sports organizations in the struggle against doping in physical training and sport.

511. The Council has the right to:

(1) consider disputes on anti-doping control in Belarus;
(2) request from state bodies the materials necessary for the activities of the Council;
(3) hear at sessions the questions of state body and federation (union, association) representatives that are within the competence of the Council;
(4) make decisions necessary for the organization, coordination and perfection of interaction between state bodies in the sphere of anti-doping control;
(5) control the performance of decisions of the Council;
(6) make decisions on the deprivation of the right of sports federations (unions, associations) to receive support in accordance with the Decree of the President of the Republic of Belarus of 15 April 2013, No. 191 'On Support to Organizations of Physical Culture and Sport' (National Legal Internet Portal of the Republic of Belarus, 17 April 2013, 1/14218), on exemption of foreign gratuitous aid from taxes and fees (duties) in accordance with the Decree of the President of the Republic of Belarus of 31 August 2015, No. 5 'On Foreign Gratuitous Aid'.[82]

82. National Legal Internet Portal of the Republic of Belarus, 3 Sep. 2015, 1/15998, including the determination of the period of validity of the applied measures.

512. Under the Council petition, scientific experts and experts of other interested organizations, including foreign organizations, into whose field of activity the struggle against doping in physical training and sport enter, can take part in its work.

513. The Chair of the Board (and in their absence – the Deputy Chair) supervises Council activity, convokes its sessions, coordinates the work of Council members and represents the Council in relations with state bodies, physical training and sports organizations and other organizations, including foreign organizations on questions relating to anti-doping politics in Belarus.

514. The decision of the Ministry of Sports and Tourism dated 11 July 2014, No. 22 (updated version: 26 June 2017, No. 22) confirms the anti-doping rules of the Republic of Belarus, the annulment of the decision of the Ministry of Sports and Tourism of the Republic of Belarus of 29 December 2004, No. 13, and a structural element of the decision of the Ministry of Sports and Tourism of the Republic of Belarus of 20 February 2008, No. 5 (hereinafter 'the Rules').[83]

515. The detection of doping in sport is the basis for the NADA or a competent international organization to consider WADA and relevant procedures, including the application (or non-application) of the relevant sanctions and/or sports disqualification. When a decision is made by an international anti-doping organization to deprive a sportsperson and other persons who have violated anti-doping rules of the right to participate in international sports competitions, a corresponding decision is made that deprives the specified persons of the right to participate in official sports competitions in Belarus and sports competitions as part of national teams of Belarus. The anti-doping organization may not demand removal of the anti-doping decision.

516. Revealing by a sportsperson the facts of use of methods and substances promoting the increase of their working capacity and forbidden for use by the legislation of Belarus and (or) decisions of the IOC or other corresponding international organizations, as well as refusal of a sportsperson to comply with anti-doping control, are a basis for carrying out anti-doping hearings.

517. The NADA of Belarus was founded according to the Order of the Ministry of Sports and Tourism of Belarus dated 7 September 2005, No. 684 'On the Creation of a National Anti-Doping Agency',[84] and the decision of the Ministerial Council of Belarus dated 27 June 2005, No. 698 'On the Creation of National Anti-Doping Agencies'.[85]

---

83. The National Register of Legal Acts of Belarus, 20 Nov. 2014, 8/29292.
84. Not published officially.
85. The National Register of Legal Acts of Belarus, 6 Jul. 2005, No. 104, 5/16192.

Chapter 3. Private Regulations

518. Regulation of the struggle against doping in sports federations is carried out on the basis of the WADA Code and norms of the relevant IF; special norms for the Belarus federations are absent.

Part IV. Sport and Commerce

Chapter 1. General Issues

519. According to Article 65 of the LPCS, physical training and sport financing are carried out at the expense of the republican and local budgets, the physical training and sports organizations and other sources that have not been forbidden by legislation. Other sources include incomes from commercial activity in a sporting sphere, such as sale of rights, tickets for sporting competitions.

Chapter 2. Public Regulations

§1. Media and Broadcasting Rights

520. All rights to the translation of sports competitions belong to the persons holding the competition if not otherwise established by the President of the Republic of Belarus, by the contract between the persons holding the competition and the participants (an organization representing the participants (or teams) or the participants in the absence of such an organization) or the regulations for conducting the sports competition (Article 45(1) LPCS).

521. Coverage of sporting events may be implemented by persons not having the right to the coverage of the sports competition in accordance with Article 45(1) of the LPCS, only with the permission of the event organizers or on the basis of an agreement on the transfer of the rights to coverage of the sports competition concluded in accordance with the law (Article 45(2) LPCS).

522. According to Article 11(4) of the Law of Belarus dated 10 May 2007, No. 225-Z (updated version: 4 January 2021) 'On Advertising',[86] the broadcasting on air or the recording of a sports competition can only be interrupted by advertising in the breaks of the sports competition or during their stops. Broadcasting on air or recording of a sports competition in which breaks or stops are not provided can be interrupted by advertising if the broadcasting interruption has not led to the loss of a part of the essential information of the sports competition.

§2. Sponsoring

I. General Rules

523. The general norms about sponsorship are contained in the Decree of the President of Belarus from 1 July 2005, No. 300 'On Granting and the Use of Gratuitous (Sponsor's) Help'[87] (updated version: 10 May 2019, No. 169). Gratuitous (sponsor's) help is given irrevocably on the basis of voluntariness and freedom in choosing its purposes according to the Decree. Requiring the granting of gratuitous (sponsor's) help is forbidden.

524. Money resources are allocated to state bodies with obligatory instructions for their target use:

(1) From the republican budget – under the order of the President of Belarus; the project of such order is, when due hereunder, brought by interested state bodies.

86. The National Register of Legal Acts of Belarus, 21 May 2007, No. 119, 2/1321.
87. The National Register of Legal Acts of Belarus, 7 Jul. 2005, No. 105, 1/6586.

(2) From the local budget – under a decision of the Minsk Executive Committee of the City Councils of People's Deputies.
(3) By granting of gratuitous (sponsor's) help, with a contract that specifies:
   (a) the organization or the individual businessperson giving the gratuitous (sponsor's) help to the addressee of such help;
   (b) the size (sum, cost calculation) of the rendered gratuitous (sponsor's) help;
   (c) the purpose of granting the gratuitous (sponsor's) help;
   (d) the kinds of goods (works, services) to be purchased using the monetary resources from the gratuitous (sponsor's) help;
   (e) an order of representation by the addressee of the gratuitous (sponsor's) help (except for addressees who are physical persons) and a report on its target use from the organization or the individual businessperson who rendered such help;
   (f) data on rendering the gratuitous (sponsor's) help in the established limits;
   (g) other conditions defined by the agreement of the parties with observance of the requirements of the Decree and other legal acts.

525. The approximate form of the contract for the granting of gratuitous (sponsor's) help is affirmed by the Council of Ministers of Belarus.

526. The contract for the granting of gratuitous (sponsor's) help, subject to coordination according to Decree No. 300, is considered in operation from the moment of its coordination; when due hereunder, other contracts for granting such help are considered in operation from the moment of their signing if not otherwise defined by the CC.

527. The organizations and individual businesspeople accepting gratuitous (sponsor's) help should present to the legal body or the individual businessperson who rendered such help a report in any form about its target use, according to Decree No. 300 and the concluded contract for the granting of gratuitous (sponsor's) help.

528. Legal bodies and the individual businesspeople providing gratuitous (sponsor's) help in the form of monetary resources can define the type of goods (works, services) that can be purchased via these means by the addressees of such help. The transfer of monetary resources without instructions on the type of goods (works, services) is not allowed.

529. The cumulative size of the gratuitous (sponsor's) help given by state bodies and other state organizations within a calendar year cannot exceed 1% of the gain received by them on realization of production (goods), works or services in the previous year of granting such help. Rendering of gratuitous (sponsor's) help by state bodies and other state organizations not receiving such gain is not limited in size.

530. Non-state legal bodies and individual businesspeople have the right to render gratuitous (sponsor's) help without size restriction. Legal bodies are obliged to provide to the state, when due hereunder, statistical reporting on the rendered gratuitous (sponsor's) help.

II. International Sponsoring

531. The rendering and use of international sponsors' help are regulated by the Decree of the President of Belarus dated 25 May 2020, No. 3 'On Foreign Free Aid' (hereinafter 'Decree No. 3').[88]

532. Foreign free aid is registered with the Department on Humanitarian Activity of the Administrative Office of the President of Belarus (hereinafter 'the Department') with statements from the recipients of foreign free aid. The forms of documents that must be submitted to the Department, a report on its use and a certificate are established by the Resolution of the Office of the President of the Republic of Belarus of 12.08.2020 No. 3 'On establishing the forms of documents'.[89] Moreover, under paragraph 5 of Decree No. 3, legal entities and individual entrepreneurs are prohibited from using foreign aid until they receive a certificate of its registration.

533. For the registration of foreign free aid legal entities and individual entrepreneurs are charged a fee of 0.5% of the amount of the assistance received, which is not exempt from taxes and fees. Free foreign aid by decision of the Office of the President of the Republic of Belarus or the Interdepartmental Commission may be exempt from the following taxes:

(1) value-added tax;
(2) income tax:
(3) tax under the simplified taxation system;
(4) single tax on individual entrepreneurs and other individuals;
(5) customs revenues for customs operations;
(6) customs duties (excluding excise goods).

534. In accordance with paragraph 13 of Decree No. 3, recipients are obliged to use free foreign aid exclusively for the purposes for which it is registered and subsequently provide a report on its use. The recipient can submit an application for changing the purposes of use, but in this case, the Interdepartmental Commission has the right to make a decision to refuse to exempt the aid from taxes and fees (duties).

88. The National Register of Legal Acts of Belarus, 25 May 2020, No. 1/19015.
89. The National Register of Legal Acts of Belarus, 25 Aug. 2020, No. 7/4571.

III. Responsibility for Illegal Sponsoring

535. Administrative responsibility for illegal sponsorship is stipulated in articles 24.14 and 24.15 of the Administrative Code of the Republic of Belarus. Article 24.14 (1) establishes that the use of foreign free aid by legal entities and individual entrepreneurs before obtaining a certificate entails the imposition of a fine in the amount of ten to thirty basic values.

536. The misuse of foreign free aid by its recipients entails the imposition of a fine in the amount of twenty to thirty basic values with the confiscation of such aid and funds received from its sale (or without confiscation). In its turn, such misuse by a legal entity entails the imposition of a fine of up to one hundred per cent of the value of the received foreign gratuitous assistance with the confiscation of such assistance and the funds received from its sale (or without confiscation) (Article 24.14 (2) of the Administrative Code).

537. Failure to deposit funds received by legal entities or individual entrepreneurs as foreign free aid to bank accounts of the Republic of Belarus within the period established by legislative acts entails the imposition of a fine in the amount of twenty to thirty basic values (Article 24.14 (3) of the Administrative Code).

538. According to Article 24.15 (1), the provision of foreign free aid by a foreign citizen or a stateless person for carrying out activities prohibited by law entails deportation with confiscation of this aid.

539. The use of foreign free aid for carrying out terrorist and other extremist activities or other acts prohibited by law, or financing political parties, unions (associations) of political parties, or preparing or holding elections, referendums, recalling deputies of the House of Representatives, members of the Council of the Republic of the National Assembly of the Republic of Belarus, deputies of the Local Council of Deputies, organizing or holding meetings, rallies, street processions, demonstrations, picketing, strikes, or the production or distribution of propaganda materials, or the organization of events aimed at conducting political and mass propaganda work among the population, entails the imposition of a fine in the amount of ten to thirty basic values with the confiscation of this aid. The commission of these actions by a legal entity entails the imposition of a fine in the amount of up to one hundred per cent of the cost of foreign free aid with its confiscation (Article 24.15 (2) of the Administrative Code).

540. If, within a year after the imposition of an administrative penalty for these actions, a person repeatedly commits them, criminal liability. As a sanction, article 369-2 of the Criminal Code of the Republic of Belarus establishes a fine, arrest or restriction of liberty for up to three years or imprisonment for up to two years.

§3. MERCHANDIZING

541. The legal bases for merchandizing in Belarus are Articles 982–985 of the CC. Article 982 of the CC 'Personal Non-property and Property Rights on Objects of Intellectual Property' establishes that the authors of the intellectual activity claim personal non-property and property rights. The personal non-property rights belong to the author, irrespective of their property rights, and remain with the author when transferring the property rights to the intellectual activity to another person.

542. Article 983 of the CC establishes exclusive rights to objects of intellectual property, including:

(1) The owner of the intellectual property rights possesses the exclusive right to lawful use of this object of intellectual property *at their own discretion in any form and any way.*
(2) Use by other persons of the objects of intellectual property, to which their legal owner possesses the exclusive right, *is allowed only with the consent of the legal owner.*
(3) The owner of the exclusive rights to the objects of intellectual property has the right to transfer this right to another person in full or in part, to allow another person the use of the object of intellectual property and to dispose of it otherwise if it does not contradict the CC or another law.

543. Restriction of exclusive rights occur in the following situations:

(1) The restriction of exclusive rights, including by granting the possibility of the use of the object of intellectual property to other persons, voiding or terminating (cancelling) the recognition of these rights are supposed in cases, limits and orders established by the CC or other laws.
(2) The restriction of exclusive rights are supposed to provide that such restrictions do not cause damage to the normal use of the object of intellectual property and do not unreasonably restrict the legitimate interests of the legal owners.
(3) Article 984 of the CC 'Transfer of Exclusive Rights to Other Persons' establishes the transfer of exclusive rights.

544. The property rights belonging to the owner of the exclusive rights to the object of intellectual property, if not otherwise provided for by the CC or other laws, can be transferred by the legal owner in full or in part to other persons under a contract and can also pass by right of succession and assignment by the reorganization of the legal person – the legal owner.

545. Transfer of property rights under a contract or their transition as universal assignment does not attract transfer or restriction of copyright and other personal non-property rights. Treaty provisions about the transfer or restriction of such rights are insignificant.

546. The exclusive rights to be transferred under a contract should be defined in it. The rights that are not specified in the contract are assumed not transferred if not otherwise proved.

547. In a contract granting exclusive rights in its action to other persons for a limited time, the rules of the licence contract (Article 985 of the CC), if not otherwise provided by law, are applied. The licence contract is an agreement on the transfer by the legal owner (licensor) of the right to the use of objects of intellectual property in the volume provided for by the contract to other persons (licensee) and includes a duty to provide to the licensor the payments specified by the contract and to carry out other actions provided by the contract.

548. Article 985 of the CC 'Licence Contract' establishes rules for the sublicense contract. This is a contract on the granting by the licensee the right to the use of the object of intellectual property to other persons within the limits defined by the licence contract. The licensee has the right to conclude the sublicense contract only in cases provided for by the licence contract. Responsibility to the licensor for actions of the sublicensee is borne by the licensee if the licence contract does not provide otherwise.

549. Article 23 of the Law of Belarus dated 5 February 1993, No. 2181-XII (updated version: 18 December 2019) 'On Trademarks and Service Marks[90] – Granting of a Licence for Trademark Use' states:

(1) The trademark right of use can be given by the owner of the trademark (licensor) to other persons (licensee) under a licence contract for all or part of the goods for which the trademark is registered;
(2) The licence contract should contain a condition that the quality of the goods of the licensee will not be below the quality of the goods of the licensor and that the licensor will carry out control over the performance of this condition.

550. Articles 17 and 18 of the law 'On Advertising' establish that placing (distribution) of advertising for alcoholic drinks, beer and soft drinks in buildings (premises, constructions) used by educational institutions, public health organizations or cultural and physical training and sports organizations is forbidden.

§4. Ownership of Clubs

551. The ownership of clubs has the same regulation as described in the previous section.

---

90. The National Register of Legal Acts of Belarus, 17 Nov. 2000, No. 106, 2/222.

§5. Betting in Sport

I. Legislation on Sports Betting

552. The activity of sports betting organizations in the Republic of Belarus is regulated by:

(1) The CC of Belarus.
(2) The Decree of the President of the Republic of Belarus dated 10 January 2005, No. 9 (updated version: 31 October 2019, No. 411) 'About the Approval of Regulations on Accomplishing Activity in the Area of the Gambling Industry in the Territory of the Republic of Belarus'.[91]
(3) The decision of the Council of Ministers of the Republic of Belarus dated 18 February 2011, No. 211 (updated version: 1 March 2019, No. 139) 'On Some Measures for Implementation of the Decree of the President of the Republic of Belarus' dated 19 November 2010, No. 599 (including 'Regulations on the Order of Keeping Casinos', 'Regulations on the Order of Keeping the Slot Machines', 'Regulations on the Order of Keeping the Pari-mutuel', 'Regulations on the Order of Keeping a Bookmaker's Office').[92]
(4) The Decree of the President of the Republic of Belarus dated 1 September 2010, No. 450 (updated version: 5 April 2021, No. 137) 'On Providing Licences for Certain Kinds of Activity'.[93]
(5) Other normative acts.

553. The CC of Belarus contains only two articles about the procedure for conducting gaming. These articles establish the grounds for the regulations on gaming. Article 932 of the CC determines that relations between organizers of totalizators and other games based on risk are accomplished in accordance with legislation and based on a contract. Such a contract between organizers and gamblers is concluded on a voluntary basis and formalized by the issue of a lottery ticket, receipt or other document or by another method stipulated by the rules of the games organizer. These principles of the CC have become the basis for the adoption of special normative acts, which regulate the activity of sports betting organizations.

554. The CC provides that the proposal to conclude a contract must include the following provisions: the terms for carrying out gaming, the procedure for determining the winner and the rate for winning. Gaming organizers must pay winnings to those who, according to the rules of sports betting, the organization concedes to be the winners. The winnings must be paid in the rate, form and term specified in the provisions for carrying out gaming. In case the terms under which the winnings must be paid are not specified, they must be paid by the sports betting organization within ten days from the moment when the demand for payment of the winnings was produced.

91. The National Register of Legal Acts of Belarus, 17 Jan. 2005, No. 5, 1/6157.
92. The National Register of Legal Acts of Belarus, 28 Feb. 2011, No. 24, 5/33363.
93. The National Register of Legal Acts of Belarus, 8 Sep. 2010, No. 212, 1/11914.

555. Article 932 of the CC also provides one of the main gambler's rights: if the gaming organizer fails to fulfil their obligation to pay the winnings, the winner has a right to claim for the payment of the winnings and compensation for damages for breach of contract caused by the organizer. The right for judicial protection is also provided for national and legal persons who while gambling or betting are affected by fraud, violence, threat or ill-intentioned agreement from a representative of the organizer of the gambling or betting. However, under Article 931 of the CC, other claims of individuals and legal persons relating to organizations of gambling and betting or related to participation in them are not subject to judicial protection in the Republic of Belarus.

556. The main normative act that determines the rules for carrying out gambling in the territory of the Republic of Belarus is the Edict of the President of the Republic of Belarus dated 10 January 2005, No. 9 (updated version: 31 October 2019, No. 411) 'On the Approval of Regulations on Accomplishing Activity in the Area of the Gambling Industry'[94] (hereinafter 'Edict No. 9'); Edict No. 9 contains definitions of the main terms, such as 'betting game', 'game of totalizator', 'totalizator' and others.

557. Bookmaker's game: a gambling game in which the participants place bets in the bookmaker's office on the results of an event (betting with the organizer of the gambling); the amount of winnings is determined before the beginning of this game and depends on partial or full coincidence of the forecast with the occurred documented facts.

558. Bookmaker's office: a gambling establishment in which the organizer of the gambling makes bets with the participants of the betting game.

559. Betting game: a gambling game in which the participants place bets in a betting pool on the forecast of the results of an event (betting with another gambling participant); the amount of winnings depends on the partial or full coincidence of the forecast with the occurred, documented facts, as well as the total amount of bets made.

560. Edict No. 9 and Resolution No. 211 determine that legal persons and sole proprietors can run betting organizations and (or) totalizators only after acquiring a licence; this licence grants special permission for exercising activity in the sphere of the gambling industry and is issued by the Ministry of Taxation. Activity relating to the running of betting organizations and (or) totalizators is exercised in a gambling establishment, the location of which is specified in the licence.

561. Gambling organizers have the right to maintain a betting office only after receiving a special permit (licence) to carry out activities in the gambling business (hereinafter 'the licence'). Betting office activities are carried out in gambling establishments, the addresses of which are specified in the licence.

---

94. 94 The National Register of Legal Acts of Belarus, 17 Jan. 2005, No. 5, 1/6157.

562. The organization and (or) holding of the gambling operation shall be carried out only by the workers of the organizer of the gambling operations.

563. Bookmakers' offices and games of chance and betting can be located in a capital structure (building, structure) and occupy this structure in whole or in part or its isolated premises, as well as in sports facilities. It is worth noting that the activities of betting and games of chance can be carried out using the global computer network of the internet.

564. Bookmaker's offices and games of chance and betting are subject to registration in a special computerized cash register system before being used by the organization and (or) for gambling.

565. Legislation of the Republic of Belarus prohibits bookmakers from taking bets from individuals who are under 18 years of age.

II. Licensing of Sports Betting Activity

566. In the Republic of Belarus, legal persons and individuals have the right to exercise certain types of activity only after receiving special permission (licence). This is on behalf of national security, public order, protection of rights and freedoms, morality, health of the population and protection of the environment. Licensing of certain types of activity provides the government with the opportunity to exercise control over the requirements for these activities.

567. The Decree of the President of the Republic of Belarus, No. 450 (updated version: 16 November 2020, No. 413)[95] 'On Licensing of Certain Types of Activity' approves in Annex 1 the list of types of activity for which special permissions (licences) are required and the list of public authorities and state organizations authorized to issue these permissions (hereinafter 'the list'). Paragraph 8 of the list mentions activities in the sphere of the gambling industry. The Ministry of Taxation is authorized for the issuance of licences in Belarus.

568. Some requirements and conditions faced by the person intending to obtain a licence are as follow:

(1) The administrator or deputy administrator of the legal entity, for whom the workplace is the principal place of business, must have a length of service in the gaming sphere, in the capacity of administrator or deputy administrator of a legal entity founded in the Republic of Belarus (with the exception of working for more than one employer) or as an individual entrepreneur registered in the territory of the Republic of Belarus, of not less than three years.

95. The National Register of Legal Acts of Belarus, 8 Sep. 2010, No. 212, 1/11914.

(2) Ownership, economic management, operational management or other legal premises necessary for the implementation of the licensed activity in accordance with the requirements of the legislation.
(3) An act of the relevant territorial authority of the interior of the place where the licensed activity is to be carried out, testifying to the absence of obstacles to the issuance of the licence.

569. The requirements and conditions for licensing according to Decree No. 450 include:

(1) Compliance with licence terms and conditions set out in paragraph 159 of the Regulations.
(2) Compliance with the requirements and conditions established by normative legal acts regulating the licensed activity, including the order of certification, maintenance of gaming equipment and registration of objects subject to gambling tax with the tax authorities.
(3) Providing:
  (a) the timely payment of the tax on gambling;
  (b) the payment of winnings (the return of unplayed rates) in accordance with the rules of gambling. In the absence of the necessary amount of cash on hand in the gambling establishment, payments must be made within twenty-four hours of services per participant's gambling winnings yield (return of unplayed rates);
  (c) protection of the gambling establishment and the safety of its visitors.
(4) Providing in the gambling establishment gaming tables, slot machines, cash registers and betting offices of bookmakers registered with the tax authorities and belonging to the licensee under the right of ownership or economic control.

570. Special licensing requirements (conditions) include the execution of works and (or) services and components of licensed activities in gambling establishments, the location of which is specified in the licence.

III. Taxation of Sports Betting Activities

571. The taxpayer in the gambling industry is a legal person of Belarus or a foreign or international organization, including those not registered as a legal person or sole proprietor, or a simple partnership (participants in a joint-venture agreement, except for participants in a consortium loan agreement) and who exercise activity in the sphere of gaming (hereinafter 'taxpayers').

572. These taxpayers are not subject to income tax, profit tax, VAT, dues for financial expenses for the maintenance and renovation of housing and dues to the local budget housing investment fund.

573. Taxpayers are obliged to keep separate accounting of income and expenses for every object for taxation.

574. The following are objects for taxation:

(1) Cash registers of a totalizator
(2) Cash registers of betting organizations.

575. Tax on the gambling industry is calculated on the assumption of the number of objects for taxation on the first date of the month under review.

576. The total number of objects for taxation is subject to obligatory registration with rating authorities. The registration is carried out after the taxpayer submits the application and until the moment the objects are installed. Rating authorities issue a certificate of registration indicating the total number of objects for taxation.

577. Registration of objects for taxation is carried out by the rating authority only if a taxpayer has special permission (licence) for exercising activity in the sphere of the gambling industry and legal acts and contracts for servicing of these objects.

578. Alteration of the total number of objects for taxation in the gambling establishment is allowed after the objects of the gambling industry are registered with the rating authority. The rating authority should issue a new certificate of registration within five working days from the date of application submission.

579. It is prohibited to keep in the gambling establishment objects for taxation that are not registered with rating authorities and (or) which do not belong to taxpayers under the rights of property. Violation of these requirements involves the abolition of the licence.

580. Rates of tax on the gambling industry are fixed in the following amounts per unit of the object of taxation:

(1) BYN 2,250 on cash registers of totalizators;
(2) BYN 1,500 on cash registers of betting organizations.

581. Tax on the gambling industry is paid under the rates fixed for the object of taxation subject to its location, in Belarusian roubles, on the assumption of the official courses fixed by the National Bank on the first date of the month under review.

582. Taxpayers submit to the rating authorities their calculation of the sum of tax on the gambling industry subject to payment in the budget before the 20th of the month following the month under review. The form of calculation is determined by the Ministry of Taxes of the Republic of Belarus. Payment of tax on the gambling industry is carried out monthly before the 22nd of the month following the month under review.

IV. Responsibility of Sports Betting Organizations

583. The Code on Administrative Infringements of the Republic of Belarus[96] (hereinafter 'the Code') determines the responsibility for the violation of the rules for gambling, for the organization and conduct of prohibited gaming and for exercising activity in the sphere of the gambling industry without a licence.

584. Article 13.6 of the Code determines that the violation of fixed rules on confirming the compliance of the playing equipment to the requirements of technical normative acts and the rules for registering the objects for taxation with the rating authorities involves amercement of the officials and legal persons, as well as seizure of the playing equipment, funds and other valuables. Violations for organizations carrying out prohibited gaming involve amercement of the officials, as well as seizure of the playing equipment, funds and other valuables.

585. Article 13.6 of the Code determines the responsibility of legal persons or sole proprietors for exercising activity in the sphere of the gambling industry without receiving special permission (licence); this involves amercement and seizure of playing equipment, funds and other valuables.

§6. Agents

I. General National Legislation

586. The principal source for the regulation of agent relations in Belarus is the CC.

587. The Belarusian CC does not contain any provisions concerning agency agreements. However, this does not mean that such relations cannot arise between persons involved in relations at civil law. According to Article 7 of the CC of Belarus, the principles governing the creation of civil rights and duties arise from the grounds provided by law, as well as from the actions of citizens and legal entities, which, although not provided by them, give rise to civil rights and obligations due to the basic principles and the meaning of civil law.

588. In accordance with this, civil rights and duties arise from agreements and other acts provided for by law and also from agreements and other acts which, although not provided for by law, nevertheless do not contradict it.

96. The National Register of Legal Acts of Belarus, 15 Jan. 2021, No. 91-3, 2/2811.

II. The Essence of an Agreement Between a Sports Agent and a Player: The Provision of Services for Remuneration

589. Nonetheless, those relations closest in terms of content to the agent's relations are those that arise within the context of a provision of services for remuneration, as regulated in Chapter 39 'The Provision of Services for Remuneration' of the Belarusian CC.

590. Under an agreement for the provision of services for remuneration, one party (the agent) is bound by the instructions of the other party (the client) to render services (perform certain acts or carry out certain activities), while the client is bound to pay for such services (Article 733(1) CC).

591. Unless otherwise provided for by an agreement for the provision of services for remuneration, the services to be performed by the agent must be personal services (Article 734 CC).

III. Procedure for Payment of Remuneration to Agents

592. The client is under an obligation to pay for the services rendered to them within the time and in the manner indicated in the agreement for the provision of services for remuneration (Article 735(1) CC).

593. In the event of impossibility of performance arising from the fault of the client, the services are subject to payment in full, save where otherwise provided for by the law on an agreement for the provision of services for remuneration (Article 735(2) CC).

594. In those cases in which impossibility of performance is due to circumstances for which neither party is responsible, the client will remunerate the agent for those expenses actually incurred by the latter, unless otherwise provided for by the law on an agreement for the provision of services for remuneration (Article 735(3) CC).

595. A unilateral refusal to perform an agreement for the provision of services for remuneration is possible under Belarusian law. According to Article 736(1) CC, a client is entitled to refuse to perform an agreement for the provision of services for remuneration on the condition that they pay the agent those expenses actually incurred by the latter. The agent is entitled to refuse to perform their obligations under an agreement for the provision of services for remuneration on the condition that they compensate the client in full for the latter's losses (Article 736(2) CC). The said rule effectively undermines the basis of sports agents' activities, inasmuch as it gives sportspeople the right to cancel the agreement with the agent at any time and with minimum compensation.

596. In accordance with Article 737 of the CC 'The Legal Regulation of Agreements for the Provision of Services for Remuneration', the general provisions on contracts (Articles 656–682) and the provisions on public utility contracts (Articles 683–695) are applicable to contracts for the provision of services for remuneration, where this does not conflict with Articles 733–736 of the Belarusian CC or the particulars of the object of an agreement for the provision of services for remuneration.

IV. Power of Attorney

597. Often, the rights of an agent to represent the interests of a player are attested by a power of attorney granted by the player. In Belarus, such power of attorney is usually given effect in the form of a notarially executed instrument.

598. Under the CC, power of attorney is a written authorization given by one party to another to represent them in dealings with third parties subject to the requirements of this article. A written authorization for the performance of certain acts by the representative may be produced directly to the third party by the party thus represented (Article 186(1) CC).

599. A power of attorney for the performance of certain acts requiring to be made in notarial form must be attested in accordance with paragraph 3 of this Article, with the exception of those cases provided for by legislative acts (Article 186(2) CC).

600. The period of validity of a power of attorney may not exceed three years. If no period of validity is indicated, it remains in force for one year reckoned from the date on which it is made. A power of attorney that contains no indication of the date on which it was made is invalid (Article 187(1) CC).

601. A notarially executed power of attorney intended for the performance of activities abroad and containing no indication of the period of validity will remain in force until revoked by the person granting it (Article 187(2) CC).

602. The person to whom the power of attorney is granted must perform in person those acts for which they are authorized. They may transfer the performance thereof to another person if authorized to do so by the power of attorney or compelled to do so by virtue of circumstances in order to defend the interests of the grantor (Article 188(1) CC).

603. A power of attorney granted by way of transfer must be notarially executed, with the exception of those cases provided for in Article 186(4) of the CC (Article 188(2) CC). The period of validity of a power of attorney granted by way of transfer may not exceed the period of validity of the power of attorney on the basis of which it was granted (Article 188(3) CC).

604. A person who has transferred authority to another must give notice of the fact to the person who granted the power of attorney and communicate to them the necessary information concerning that person to whom the authority has been transferred.

Failure to perform this obligation imposes on the party transferring the authority a liability for the acts of that person to whom they have transferred the authority, as though such acts were their own (Article 188(4) CC).

605. The validity of a power of attorney is terminated as a consequence of:

(1) expiry of the period of validity;
(2) revocation of the power of attorney by the person granting it;
(3) refusal on the part of the person to whom it was granted;
(4) discontinuation of the juridical person in whose name the power of attorney was granted;
(5) discontinuation of the juridical person to whom the power of attorney was granted;
(6) the death of the person who granted the power of attorney or a declaration to the effect that they have died, that they have become (legally) incapable or partly incapable or that they are absent and their whereabouts are unknown;
(7) the death of the person to whom the power of attorney was granted, or a declaration to the effect that they have died, that they have become incapable or partly incapable or that they are absent and their whereabouts are unknown (Article 189(1) CC).

606. A person who has granted a power of attorney may at any time revoke or transfer the power of attorney; the person to whom the power of attorney has been granted may refuse it. The power of attorney may be cancelled by the person who issued it (Article 189(2) CC). The validity of a transfer is lost with the termination of the power of attorney (Article 189(3) CC).

607. A person who has granted but subsequently revoked a power of attorney is obliged to give notice of such revocation to that person to whom the power of attorney was granted and to any third parties in respect of which persons the power of attorney was granted to represent them (Article 190(1) CC).

608. The rights and duties arising as a result of the activities of that person to whom the power of attorney has been granted, before such person knew or ought to have known of the termination thereof, remain in force for the person who has granted the power of attorney and their successors at law in their relations with third parties. This rule is not applied in the event that the third party knew or ought to have known that the validity of the power of attorney had been terminated (Article 190(2) CC). Upon the termination of a power of attorney, the successors at law of the person to whom it has been granted are obliged to immediately return the power of attorney (Article 190(3) CC).

609. In the event that the power of attorney has been granted abroad or granted to a foreign player or to a foreign agent, such power of attorney will be regulated by the rules of private international law contained in the CC of the Republic of Belarus. The form and period of validity of the power of attorney are defined by the law of that country in which the power of attorney was granted. However, a power of attorney may not be declared invalid as a result of non-observance of the form if the latter satisfies the requirements of the law of the Republic of Belarus (Article 1117).

V. Procedural Rights of Sports Agents

610. It is a feature of the activity of a sports agent in Belarus that the agent, not being a lawyer, cannot represent the interests of the player in courts of ordinary jurisdiction, a fact that flows from the provisions of Article 72 of the Code of Civil Procedure[97] (CCP) 'Persons Who May Appear as Representatives in Court'.

611. A person may appear as a representative in court if he/she is capable, being in possession of an appropriately formulated authority to conduct the case in court, with the exception of those persons listed in Article 73 of the CCP.

612. The following persons may appear as representatives in court:

(1) advocates;
(2) persons in the service of juridical persons in matters concerning such persons;
(3) authorized persons acting on behalf of public associations (organizations legally empowered to represent and defend in the courts the rights and legal interests of members of such public associations, organizations and other persons);
(4) authorized organizations that have been granted a legal right to represent and defend in the courts the rights and legal interests of other persons;
(5) legal representatives;
(6) close relations, husband (wife);
(7) representatives appointed by the court;
(8) one of the legal associates – acting on the instructions of such associates;
(9) patent attorneys.

613. However, in the event that an agent represents a foreign player in a Belarusian court, the agent must act in accordance with the rules of international civil action contained in section X of the CCP. The rules contained in this section are more liberal in relation to the representing of foreigners in the courts. According to Article 551 of the CCP 'Representation in International Civil Actions', when conducting cases in the courts of the Republic of Belarus, foreign citizens and legal persons are entitled freely and without hindrance to avail themselves of the services of

97. The National Register of Legal Acts of Belarus, 17 Mar. 1999, Nos 18–19, 2/13.

both foreign representatives, including advocates, and representatives, including advocates, from Belarus. In civil legal proceedings, foreign representatives, including advocates, have the same rights and acquire the same duties as representatives, including advocates, from Belarus.

Chapter 3. Private Regulations

614. Private regulations of the sporting sphere are based on the autonomy of sports-related bodies that constitute *lex sportiva*. The most powerful federations from a financing point of view are football (soccer), ice hockey, basketball, handball and tennis. These federations possess documents on the regulation of commercial activity. However, these documents are closed.

§1. Private Regulations for Financing in Tennis

615. Nevertheless, the author finds it necessary to consider in this section a sample of private regulations for internal financing in the framework of the Belarusian Tennis Federation. The tennis federation has regulations on the financing of the statutory activities that determine the order of financing sportspeople, coaches and referees by the federation.

I. Terminology

616. In order to ensure uniform and accurate application of the terms used in these provisions, the following definitions are supplied:

(1) *International Tennis Federation* (ITF).
(2) *European Tennis Association* (ETA).
(3) *Federation* – Republican Public Association (RPA), Belarusian Tennis Federation (BTF);
(4) *Official* – worker in a Federation, ITF or ETA, coach, foreign referees and their assistants and other persons being in a contractual relationship or other official relations with the Federation, ITF or ETA (besides sportspeople and technical staff).
(5) *Competition* – the championships, Belarus Cup tournaments and other competitions among sportspeople under the auspices of the Federation and/or the ITF and ETA.
(6) *Sportspeople* – individuals who regularly play tennis, constantly enhance their athletic skills and regularly take part in tennis competitions and training camps; individuals who cease to participate in tennis competitions but continue to receive income directly in connection with participation in sports competitions in the past.
(7) *Sports activity* – the activity of sportspeople aimed at participation in a competition, as well as other activities indirectly related to participation in competitions that involve a sportsperson obtaining income from advertising and/or sponsorship.
(8) *Referee* – a citizen of the Republic of Belarus authorized by the Federation to monitor compliance with the rules of tennis competitions, to determine the winners and to record the sports results.

(9) *Technical staff* – persons who are not officials and not included in the protocol of the competition but participate in the preparation and organization of tennis competitions under the auspices of the Federation and/or the ITF and ETA by performing technical and support functions.

(10) *Coach* – Specialist on sportsperson training who performs training work to educate, train and improve skills and develop the functionality of sportspeople.

617. The Contract of Financing is a contract between the Federation and the sportsperson on the financing of the competitive or training activity of the sportsperson, according to which the Federation is obliged to provide the sportsperson with the means (assets) in the agreed amount and by the due date, and the sportsperson agrees to reimburse the means transferred under the contract at the expense of the revenues from sports activities undertaken in the contract period. For simplicity, all references in the text of the Regulations on the nouns of the masculine gender include both men and women, and all plural nouns apply equally to nouns in the singular. The Regulations on the principles and procedure of financing of the statutory activities of the Federation (hereinafter 'the Regulations'), developed in accordance with the Law of the Republic of Belarus 'On Physical Culture and Sports' and the Charter of the Federation, define the order of allocation, distribution and spending of earmarked funds (cash, financial, material) to maintain prospective and talented sportspeople – members of the Federation – in training and competitive activities, to finance the activities of coaches, referees and other officials for the purpose of participation in tennis competitions and to engage in economic activities not prohibited by legislation. The Regulations do not regulate wages and other payments to employees under labour relations.

618. Financing in this provision includes the provision of wealth within the statutory activities of the Federation (including but not limited to the provision of sports equipment, sports clothing and shoes).

619. The Regulations must be applied by the Federation, its representatives, sportspeople, coaches, referees and officials. Any bilateral written document (contract) on financing under the Regulations shall contain a reference to the application of the Regulations.

II. Principles of Financing

620. Legality: Spending of own funds and loan proceeds shall be in accordance with the laws of the Republic of Belarus and the Charter of the Federation.

621. Repayment: In cases when the financing of a sportsperson includes the principal of the sportsperson who received such financing returning such financing (or part of the financing) to the Federation if they win a sports competition and receive income from it.

622. Goal using: Funds provided for the statutory purposes of the Federation in accordance with the Regulations shall be used solely for the purposes for which they were sent.

623. The distribution of risks: The Federation shall consider the risks associated with the action of the force majeure factors that caused the need for additional financing (delay of vehicles, delay of the competition). The burden of proving the existence of force majeure factors are on the subject of financing.

624. Current control: Spending of the funds is subject to current control. Control over the use of funds may be held by the chief accountant of the Federation, the Federation Audit Commission and/or the members of the management bodies. Any financing of the statutory activities of the Federation shall be accompanied by a report on the use of the funds under applicable law and shall be provided at least once a month unless otherwise established by the decisions on financing or the contract of financing. The report is provided to the Executive Director of the Federation by the person receiving the budget financing. In the case of financing under a contract for services, the report is filed in the form of the act on the provision of services signed by the parties.

III. Sources of Financing

625. The sources of financing are the Federation's own funds, as well as loan proceeds and means transferred by sponsors of the Federation.

626. The Federation is not entitled to finance if it operates at a loss.

IV. Subjects of Financing

A. Sportspeople

627. Only sportspeople who are members of the Federation can receive financing on the basis of the contract of financing under this Regulation. Termination of membership in the Federation does not cancel the contract of financing of the sportsperson concluded at the time of their membership.

628. Offers for the conclusion of a contract of financing is formalized by the sportsperson (or by their representative) in the form of a written statement (application) sent to the Federation.

629. The application for the conclusion of a contract of financing is considered at a meeting of the Bureau of the Board within one month from the date of receipt of the application; the contract is drawn according to protocol and signed by all participants of the meeting of the Bureau of the Board of the Federation.

630. Decisions on the conclusion of a contract of financing can be made based on the written conclusions about the potential of the sportsperson issued by the Coach Council of the Federation, signed by not less than two members of the Coach Council (Chair and Secretary).

B. Coaches

631. Coaches receive financial support under the contract of paid services by a coach, a model of which is given in Annex B to the Regulations.

632. Decisions on the conclusion of a contract of paid services by a coach are adopted by the Bureau of the Federation. The contract of paid services by a coach is signed on behalf of the Federation by the President of the Federation or a person authorized by power of attorney.

C. Referees

633. Referees receive financing from the Federation in accordance with the rates of pay set by legislation. If the referee fulfils additional types of works (services) for the Federation aimed at the realization of its statutory goals, they may be paid on the basis of the relevant turnkey contracts (service contracts).

D. Officials

634. Officials who are not on the staff of the Federation do not receive payment under service contracts in accordance with the civil legislation.

635. The issue of concluding a contract for the payment of an official's services is within the competence of the Executive Director of the Federation.

E. Technical Personnel

636. Technical personnel not part of the staff of the Federation may receive remuneration under service contracts in accordance with the civil legislation.

637. The issue of concluding a contract for the payment of an official's services is within the competence of the Executive Director of the Federation.

V. Objects of Financing

638. Objects of financing are:

(1) contributions for a sportsperson's participation in competitions;
(2) use of franchises, trademarks and service marks for the organization of competitions;
(3) activities aimed at popularizing tennis;
(4) entertainment expenses;
(5) the acquisition of modern medical drugs and food additives (allowed to use);
(6) accommodation and meals during training workshops (schools) on tennis;
(7) accommodation and meals while attending the event (living expenses);
(8) promotional activities for the organization of competitions;
(9) sports nutrition;
(10) life, health and property insurance of the Federation;
(11) Souvenirs and official symbols of Federation competitions and competitions held under its auspices;
(12) travel costs for competitions;
(13) medical services;
(14) officials' services;
(15) coaches' services;
(16) sports equipment.

639. Living expenses for participation in competitions, including travel to the places holding the competition, are planned on the basis of norms established by the Ministry of Finance of the Republic of Belarus. Living expenses may be increased by a decision of the Bureau of the Federation; the decision to increase living expenses must be justified.

640. Entertainment expenses in accordance with the Regulations include the organization of meetings, conferences, seminars, and councils, the conducting of business receptions by the leader of the Federation, by the Bureau of the Board of the Federation and by the Executive Director of the Federation, organizing the honouring of sportspeople and receiving foreign delegations and accompanying persons (accommodation, meals, cultural events, gifts (souvenirs) with symbols of the Federation, household services, translation services and transportation services).

641. Sportspeople, coaches, officials or employees of the Federation may apply in writing for financing to the Bureau of the Board of the Federation. Applications for financing must include the following documents:

(1) A reasonable opinion on the influence of the proposed measures and resources, such as on improving athletic performance of sportspeople in competitions.
(2) Calculation of costs for participation in competitions.
(3) Substantiation of price conditions of the application.
(4) Substantiation of the selection of the supplier or contractor.

VI. Dispute Resolution

642. All disputes in connection with the application of the Regulations after failure to reach an agreement for one month from the date of the first claims filed by a party to the dispute shall be referred to the Sports Arbitration Court at the 'Belarusian Republican Union of Jurists' in Minsk, with the exception of the jurisdiction of the state courts.

643. The decision of the Sports Arbitration Court at the PA 'Belarusian Republican Union of Jurists' is final and binding for the parties.

Chapter 4. The Impact of COVID-19 on Sport

644. The situation with COVID-19 was common for all kinds of sports competitions of the national level, so we limit our explanation showing the impact on football.[98] Although there have been non-significant postponements because of players' contacts with COVID-19 carries, the 2019-2020 professional football season had been completed due to the schedule by December 2020. It was quite a unique football league of the world active that year. The 2020-2021 season started in March 2021 and ended with no restrictions due to the pandemic.

645. Since Belarus has not implemented any special strict measures due to COVID-19, all subjects to Belarusian sport are guided by the general recommendations. Mostly, there are general recommendations that shall be applied by all subjects to football sport. Thus, the Sports and Tourism Ministry of the Republic of Belarus has instructed sports organizations and federations to take the following measures:

- permit regime determination to sports premises;
- space separation of athletes and engaged in physical activities individuals' as well as minimization of their contacts;
- the centralized team hosting with sanitary-epidemiological regime compliance.

At national level football matches, there are no restrictions on attendance at stadia. As a result, supporters are allowed to attend games in compliance with general safety measures.

The Belarusian Football Federation has developed the additional measures to those taken by the Sports and Tourism Ministry of the Republic of Belarus:

- sanitizer dispensers installation in the lobbies and administration premises floors, at the sports premise entrance;
- holding of moist mopping twice a day with the use of disinfectants;
- monitoring of players' and football employees' physical well-being and informing the Belarusian Football Federation on any COVID-19 case.

The Football Federation of Belarus has posted on its official website the main principles of preventive COVID-19 treatment made by FIFA. That has been said the main measure is the development of the level of social responsibility. As a result, a range of informing meetings for players have been held.

All football activities have been going on with some modifications on health security. In order to minimise risks, the Belarusian Football Federation and Sports and Tourism Ministry of the Republic of Belarus have recommended all football clubs and competition organizers to take the following measures:

98. *See also*: Zhurava Maryia. COVID-19 and Its Impact on Football – A Sports Law and Policy Centre and LawInSport Joint Survey – 4th Edition. – Belarus. // https://www.lawinsport.com/topics/covid19-impact/item/coronavirus-a-and-its-impact-on-football-a-sports-law-and-policy-centre-and-lawinsport-joint-survey-2.

- spectators' seating in chessboard order;
- fans flow division within sports premises' entrances;
- fans' temperature measurement with thermal sights;
- spectators' informing on the application of sanitary-epidemiological measures, including throughout information COVID-19 board.

As the relations between clubs, on the one side, and players, coaches or staff, on the other side, are stipulated with labour law, all the employees are obliged to be at work and comply with work regulations unless stated otherwise. Clubs, in their turn, shall ensure a safe working environment. Herewith all changes to the regime, time, place of work could take place only with the mutual employer-employee agreement. Players, coaches and staff are entitled to ask for social leaves. Taking into account the problematic epidemiological situation, such leaves are likely to be granted. There are no legal grounds for the suspension of payment of salary for COVID-19 reasons. However, due to the problematic pandemic situation, clubs have had to cut salaries.

No specific measures have been taken by the Government on the issue of unemployment or any other benefits application due to COVID-19. However, the President Decree on general economic support during the pandemic has been adopted.[99] The Decree clubs that rent the state-owned premises have the right to ask for a postponement of payment.

The Belarusian Football Federation, as other sports federations, has not introduced any common funding or taken any specific measures to support clubs financially. However, the Football Federation of Belarus is planning to support clubs with the grants provided by FIFA.

646. The concept of 'force majeure' is introduced in civil law relations only and not in labour relations. Neither 'force majeure' concept nor exemption from liability due to any insuperable circumstances can be applied by the employer. Under the labour regulations, the employer is entitled to adopt only the concept of production necessity. Due to production necessity, the rights of the employments are limited. For instance, the employer can transfer the employee to another department or even to another employer. Nonetheless, the employer cannot delay, suspend or cut salary payments.

647. There have been no dramatic developments relating to agreements with broadcasters. In fact, the situation is quite the opposite: since the Belarusian football championships were the only football competitions that were held, the Football Federation of Belarus has had the possibility to increase revenue from broadcasting.

648. The Football Federation of Belarus has not met any significant problems with sponsors' support. At the same time, the situation with the clubs is different: clubs' sponsors had to reduce funding.

99. Edict of the President of the Republic of Belarus of 24.04.2020 No 143 'On support of the economy' / National Legal Internet Portal of the Republic of Belarus, 25 Apr. 2020, 1/18970.

Selected Bibliography

Danilevich, A. 'Country Reports – Belarus/Player's Agents Worldwide'. In *Legal Aspects*, ed. R.C.R. Siekmann, R. Parrish, R. Branco Martins & J. Soek. The Hague: T.M.C. Asser Press, 2007, 91–104.

Danilevich, A.S. Ponyatie sportivnogo pravootnosheniya. / A.S.Danilevich// VestnikVyssh. Hoz. Suda Resp. Belarus'. – 2010. – No. 7. – S.139–141.

Danilevich, A.S. Ponyatienacional'nogo i mejdunarodnogosportivnogo prava / Aktual'nyeproblemymejdunarodnogopublichnogo i mejdunarodnogochastnogoprava: sb. nauch. tr. Vyp. 1/redkol.: E.V. Babkina, Yu. A. Lepeshkov (otv. Redaktory) [i dr.]. – Minsk: BGU, 2009, – S. 250–264.

Danilevich, A.S., Kapskaya A.A. Ponyatie mejdunarodnogo perehoda (transfera) sportmena. / A.S. Danilevich, A.A. Kapskaya//Vestnik Vyssh. Hoz. Suda Resp. Belarus'. – 2010. – No. 10. – S. 152–155.

Kamenkov, V.S. Nacional'noe sportivnoe pravo Belarusi: ponyatie, realii i V. Kamenkov//Vestnik Vysshego Hozyaistvennogo Suda Respubliki Belarus'. – 2009. – No. 10. – S. 141–151.

Kamenkov, V.S. Ponyatie i razreshenie sportivnyh sporov v mire i v Belarusi V. Kamenkov//Yusticiya Belarusi. – 2009. – No. 6. – S. 34–36.

Kamenkov, V.S. Pravovye problemy v deyatel'nosti belorusskih sportivnyh sudei// Vestnik Vysshego Hozyaistvennogo Suda Respubliki Belarus'. – 2009. – No. 16. – S. 143–151.

Kamenkov, V.S. Trudovaya li funkciya–deyatel'nost' professional'nogo sportmena ? //Vestnik Vysshego Hozyaistvennogo Suda Respubliki Belarus '. – 2009. – No. 15. – S. 143–150.

Sportivnoe pravo v Respublike Belarus': sb. st.sost. red. jurn. 'Promyshlenno-torgovoe pravo'. – Minsk: Red. jurn. 'Promyshlenno-torgovoe pravo', 2011. – 288 s.

Sportivnoye pravo Respubliki Belarus': uchebnoye posobiye / V.S. Kamenkov [i dr.]; pod red. V.S. Kamenkova. – Minsk: Chetyre chetverti, 2019. – 422 s.

Sportivnoye pravo: uchebnoye posobiye dlya studentov uchrezhdeniy vysshego obrazovaniya po spetsial'nosti 'Pravovedeniye' / A. YU. Lomako. – Minsk: Vysheyshaya shkola, 2017. – 207 s.

Sportivnoye pravo / A. N. Simchuk. – Minsk: Amalfeya, 2020. – 482 s.

Sportivnoye pravo Respubliki Belarus' / V. A. Kruglov. – Minsk: Amalfeya, 2018. – 246 s.

Sportivnoye agentirovaniye / Sergey Il'ich. – Beau Bassin [Bo-Bassen Rozkhill]: LAP Lambert Academic Publishing, cop. 2018. – 50 s.

Selected Bibliography

Sportivnoye pravo v Respublike Belarus' [Elektronnyy resurs]: sbornik statey / Ministerstvo sporta i turizma Respubliki Belarus' [i dr.]. – Minsk: Redaktsiya zhurnala 'Promyshlenno-torgovoye pravo', 2016

Sportivnoye pravo v Respublike Belarus' [Elektronnyy resurs] / Ministerstvo sporta i turizma Respubliki Belarus' [i dr.]. Vyp. 7. – 2017. – 1 elektronnyy opticheskiy disk (CD-ROM)

Sportivnoye pravo v Respublike Belarus' [Elektronnyy resurs] / Ministerstvo sporta i turizma Respubliki Belarus' [i dr.]. Vyp. 8. – 2018. – 1 elektronnyy opticheskiy disk (CD-ROM)

Sportivnoye pravo v Respublike Belarus' [Elektronnyy resurs] / Ministerstvo sporta i turizma Respubliki Belarus' [i dr.]. Vyp. 9. – Minsk: YurSpektr, 2019. – 1 elektronnyy opticheskiy disk (CD-ROM)

Sportivnoye pravo v Respublike Belarus' [Elektronnyy resurs] / Ministerstvo sporta i turizma Respubliki Belarus' [i dr.]. Vyp. 10. – Minsk: YurSpektr, 2020. – 1 elektronnyy opticheskiy disk (CD-ROM)

Tomashevski, K.L. Aktual'nye voprosy sootnosheniya trudovogo i sportivnogo prava v Belarusi i Rossii Sport: ekonomika, pravo, upravlenie. – 2007. – No. 3. – S.12–15.

Index

The numbers here refer to paragraph numbers.

Index

www.ingramcontent.com/pod-product-compliance
Ingram Content Group UK Ltd.
Pitfield, Milton Keynes, MK11 3LW, UK
UKHW020146290926
15471UKWH00004B/713

9 789403 549118